Samuel
Johnson
the
Moralist

SAMUEL
JOHNSON
THE
MORALIST

Robert Voitle

HARVARD UNIVERSITY PRESS
Cambridge, Massachusetts
1961

*Publication of this book has been aided
by grants from the Ford Foundation and
from the Research Council of the
University of North Carolina*

Distributed in Great Britain by Oxford University Press, London

Printed in the United States of America
Library of Congress Catalog Card Number: 61–8842

To George Sherburn

PREFACE

At the conclusion of an essay wherein he has discussed the theories of some of the most renowned English philosophers, the author of the "History of the Science of Morals" which appeared in the 1797 edition of the *Encyclopaedia Britannica* refers to Samuel Johnson as "the first moralist of the age." We are not accustomed to giving Johnson precedence over such theoreticians as Berkeley, Bishop Butler, Hume, nor even over less original writers such as Shaftesbury and Paley; nor is it clear to us why many of Johnson's contemporaries did so. A principal reason why we do not fully appreciate Johnson's appeal to his own century is that only certain parts of his moral thought interest us; much of the rest is little regarded because we have sought other solutions to problems which Johnson considered moral. And the noses of so many deterministic camels have been admitted to our tent that even if we wished to, none of us could now be perpetually a moralist as Johnson was. It follows that the best way to get a comprehensive view of Johnson's moral notions is to disregard our particular interests and needs and to consider these notions in the terms of his own century. That is what I intend to do in this essay, though I can only hope to make a beginning.

Maintaining objectivity is the great problem in such a study. A careful investigation of the history of Johnson's reputation would reveal that while we have been gradually learning more of the truth about him, we have also created a succession of different Johnsons, each of these images reflecting the tastes and opinions of the age which conceived it. Some of the differences between these various Johnsons were the result of selecting from the original, others arose from distortion. One can hardly question the legitimacy of this process of selection and distortion, for it is the way in which most figures of the past retain a vital influence upon succeeding generations, but its effects certainly should be kept to a minimum here.

There would be little need to worry about such a process seriously affecting this portrait of Johnson as a moralist, were it possible to portray him against a broad background of the thought of his age. This is not feasible because the painting of such a background is in itself too ambitious a project, and could it be painted, it would inevitably distract attention from the figure before it. Leslie Stephen's history of English thought in the eighteenth century remained standard for many years largely on account of its excellence, but now it persists chiefly because scholars are intimidated by the magnitude and the complexity of the task of replacing it.

There are a number of devices short of a full background which can at least help us get a more objective view of Johnson the moralist, and although the use of these devices may at times make the early part of the essay seem rather broadly focused, they should assure that some degree of perspective is maintained when the picture narrows down to Johnson alone, as it soon does. One of the commonest pitfalls of intellectual history is the fact that terms remain the same while their meanings change. Accordingly, the more important definitions should be illustrated as much as possible from other writers of the day, so that they will be seen in the proper perspective. It will also help to compare Johnson's notions from time to time with those of thinkers who were more systematic, and whose relationship to the general history of thought is more easily seen. I have chosen John Locke and Bishop Cumberland for this purpose because, directly or indirectly, both of them strongly influenced Johnson's moral thinking.

I hope that my rather profuse documentation will be forgiven as another device to promote objectivity. The further away a man is in time, the easier it becomes to distort his thought by seizing upon isolated statements which seem to accord with our own pet notions. Johnson is especially vulnerable in this respect because he has influenced the thinking of most of his partisans in one way or another, and we are reluctant to admit that a man who has profoundly influenced us may think in a wholly different spirit from us with regard to most matters. We like to feel that the differences which we see are due only to the accidents of time and place. Systematic treatment of Johnson's ideas would seem to be advisable, too, and there is no need to apologize for it. Though Johnson is not at all systematic, his moral thought is impressively consistent when seen wholly, and in the context of his times.

By documenting extensively one is also better able to allow for Johnson's constantly shifting personae. As a practical moralist and a neoclassic author he is always aware of the occasion, of his purposes, and of the nature of his audience. In the case of a systematic philosopher, if we take into account any change in his ideas with time, we usually are safe in regarding his utterances as a continuous fabric in which the pattern of his thoughts can be discerned, but it would be folly indeed to lump together indiscriminately the preacher *in absentia* at Ashbourne, the raconteur of the Club, the anguished sinner of the *Prayers and Meditations,* the biographer, the lexicographer, the sober moralist of the *Ramblers,* and the sometimes sportive bear of Streatham. There is the further complication that Johnson, or for that matter, any practical moralist, speaks primarily not to inform his audience, as the theoretician does, but to reform their actions. Although this gives him no license to engage in sophistry, he can legitimately judge truth with respect to its formative effects instead of treating it as some body of absolute data to be expounded from a uniform point of view. He can select portions of the truth and stress them to whatever degree the occasion may demand. The safest course, then, is to assume that we are always confronted by a persona and that we must continually be vigilant with respect to the context in which ideas occur and the frequency of their occurrence.

Because Johnson the moralist is single-mindedly devoted to the practical task of reformation, some of the aspects of his thought which I will consider may seem novel, perhaps annoyingly so, even to readers well acquainted with Johnson. In part, this air of novelty is caused by the difference between the values we find in Johnson and those admired by his contemporaries. Just as responsible is the fact that we must occasionally look behind Johnson's practical statements into areas of his thinking best described as his silences—not the subconscious strata of his psyche which have fascinated some modern investigators, but rather into realms of conscious knowledge in which Johnson is competent and sometimes expert, yet concerning which he says little.

He said and wrote so much, and so much of this has been preserved, that we are prone to assume that we have a fairly complete picture of his intellectual experience. In reality, we sometimes see only the top of the iceberg; our vision is limited to what the occasion on which he is speaking requires or it is restricted by the pattern of Boswell's intellectual preoccupations. In some instances we have the testimony of others as to how much lies below the surface. For example, most of those who knew Johnson will testify to his admiration for the theological writings of Samuel Clarke, but who can trace the influence of Clarke on his thought? It might be possible to explain the allusions to Clarke and to many others by arguing that one can esteem an author without absorbing his thought or even knowing his thought well, were it not for the case of Richard Hooker. Neither Boswell nor

Mrs. Thrale so much as record the mention of his name, but we know from the hundreds of citations in the *Dictionary* that Johnson was in fact intimately acquainted with Hooker's writings.

Often Johnson himself gives us a glimpse of how much lies below the surface, by speaking out on some uncustomary topic in a way which clearly shows that he has devoted much thought to the matter. When these glimpses are offered to us unexpectedly, as frequently they are, they seem to prove that Johnson was silent on some topics for the simple reason that he seldom had proper opportunity to speak on them and demonstrate his competency. For instance, his most astute remarks upon the relation of positive law to natural law were made while he was feasting on Scotch broth at an Aberdeen dinner table. Again, all of his political tracts are polemic and make an inappropriate setting for a statement of fundamental political theory. To find this statement, we must turn, oddly enough, to the *Sermons*.

Other topics he had sufficient opportunity to discuss, but failed to do so for reasons that are not always clear. Thus, despite Boswell's pronounced thirst for what he calls "intellectual conversation," he was not able to garner a drop of what justly can be called metaphysical discussion for his huge biography. And Johnson himself supplied rather extensive annotations for his translation of Crousaz's metaphysical treatise without ever commenting on this aspect of the work. Yet his review of Soame Jenyns's *Free Enquiry into the Origin and Nature of Evil* shows how well he can argue on such a subject, and it affords us another proof of how far beyond his common topics of conversation Johnson's interests range.

It is easier to account for some of the topics I will treat than it is to justify the categorical fashion in which most of what I have to say is delivered. My *ex cathedra* manner is not due to lack of humility, nor—formidable as that task is—does it stem from despair of taking into account and properly acknowledging the voluminous scholarship relevant to some of the topics I discuss. It is simply that the subject itself all too readily leads one into perpetual qualifications and endless antitheses. One must choose between plowing straight ahead or attending to all the nuances and rapidly sinking into obscurity. I hope that a blanket apology here will make my choice of the first of these alternatives more acceptable.

This study has been published with the generous assistance of the Research Council of the University of North Carolina and the Ford Foundation. I am especially grateful to George Sherburn, W. J. Bate, James L. Clifford, Benjamin Boyce, and J. O. Bailey for their very helpful suggestions. My indebtedness to my wife is manifold and great.

R. V.

CONTENTS

Samuel
Johnson
the
Moralist

ABBREVIATIONS

Journey	*Johnson's Journey to the Western Islands of Scotland* and *Boswell's Journal of a Tour to the Hebrides,* edited by R. W. Chapman (Oxford, 1924).
Letters	*The Letters of Samuel Johnson,* edited by R. W. Chapman (3 vols.; Oxford, 1952).
Life	*Boswell's Life of Johnson,* edited by George Birkbeck Hill, revised by L. F. Powell (6 vols.; Oxford, 1934–1950).
Lives	*Lives of the English Poets by Samuel Johnson, LL.D.,* edited by George Birkbeck Hill (3 vols.; Oxford, 1905).
Misc.	*Johnsonian Miscellanies,* edited by George Birkbeck Hill (2 vols.; Oxford, 1897).
Poems	*The Poems of Samuel Johnson,* edited by David Nichol Smith and Edward L. McAdam (Oxford, 1941).
Thraliana	*Thraliana: The Diary of Mrs. Hester Lynch Thrale (Later Mrs. Piozzi) 1776–1809,* edited by Katharine C. Balderston (2 vols.; Oxford, 1942).
Works	*The Works of Samuel Johnson, LL.D.* (9 vols.; Oxford, 1825).

$\mathcal{E}$ I $\mathcal{3}$

Reason and Empiricism

Reason is the foundation upon which Johnson's moral concepts are built, and unless from the outset we understand the nature of his rationalism, our analysis of his moral notions will be a tottering and insecure structure. Unfortunately, most of what has been said about Johnson's attitude toward reason is of little help to us because his rationalism has not been described in its historical context. One cannot proceed very far with an investigation of his psychological and ethical assumptions without sensing the tension which exists between Johnson and his intellectual environment. Professor Bertrand Bronson's portrayal of Johnson swimming vigorously against the current of political thought also describes his situation with respect to contemporary trends in moral psychology. To know what Johnson means, we must know what he is reacting against, for, as R. G. Collingwood has shown, answers are meaningless if we do not know accurately the questions to which they refer.

Scholars have hesitated to depict Johnson's rationalism against the background of its historical context because the context itself appears blurred. What did *reason* mean when the *Ramblers* were being written? Certainly the sometimes useful assumption that Johnson's contemporaries all intend the same thing—common sense, for instance—when they speak of the rational faculty will not serve us here. Johnson himself acknowledges the wide variety of possible meanings by his choice of illustrations in the *Dictionary*. The faculty which Richard Hooker can confidently describe as "the director of man's will, discovering in action what is good" because "the laws of well-doing are the dictates of right reason" is obviously different from the faculty whose "glimmering ray," Dryden tells us, was not intended "to assure our doubtful way." Nor is it likely that Sir John Davies and John Locke would agree as to how the reason functions, yet Johnson cites them both. It is not surprising that we now find these various denotations of *reason* hard to unravel. The best approach for the purposes of this essay will be to confine ourselves strictly to those eighteenth-century concepts of the rational faculty which are relevant to moral theory and describe them briefly in historical terms, then relate Johnson's rationalism to them.

Two relevant concepts of the rational faculty prevailed during Johnson's day—although there are many subdivisions under each heading. The most prevalent of the two concepts I will call Lockean reason. This is an awkward term, but, while Locke deserves no credit for originating the concept, he was its most influential exponent. Furthermore, this way I will not be thought fond of oxymoron, as I might be, were I to designate it more precisely, as "empirical reason." Under the other general species we will lump together all survivals of the traditional notion of reason according to the faculty psychology and call this species Peripatetic reason although this term is also a compromise, since included are notions which originated neither with Aristotle nor with the scholastics.

Let us first consider the older Peripatetic species. In order to do so we must glance back at the faculty psychology which last flourished during the reign of Elizabeth, because this concept of reason owes its nature to the purposes it served in that venerable theory of human nature, which derived ultimately from Aristotle, was elaborated by the medieval scholastics, and further modified by the philosophers and theologians of the Renaissance. By the sixteenth century, so many permutations and combinations had evolved, that the faculty psychology is best thought of as a cluster of theories having the same general outline—authorities of the period constantly disagree regarding details. The subject of the discipline is not mind but soul, the vital spiritual principle or substance from which spring all the functions, from the highest to the lowest, which differentiate man from a stone or a lifeless piece of wood. On the basis of these functions, the soul is divided into three sections, which should be thought of as parts of a general harmony, not as separate entities. The most humble part, the vegetative soul, governing nutrition, growth, and reproduction, is also possessed by plants and animals. In man, it is the source of the instinctive drives and appetites which serve the body's most fundamental needs. More complex is the sensitive soul, shared with animals but not possessed by plant life. This soul is the seat of motion and sensation, and, in general, it mediates between the individual and his environment. In addition to the five senses, its most important faculties are the emotions, the memory, and the imagination. Emotions, sensitive appetites, are primarily intended to protect the organism from external dangers and to enable it to profit from advantageous situations. Accordingly, in their most primitive form they represent a drawing back of the soul from what seems immediately harmful, and an attraction toward those objects of sensation which seem beneficial or pleasurable. Memory stores the images provided by the senses, and imagination combines the various images of sensation or those drawn from the memory and proffers them to the reason—

images which may also produce an emotional reaction. Reason's seat is the rational soul, which man shares only with the angels and with God. The prime function of this, the supreme faculty of the soul is to analyze and evaluate the data of experience, to choose and plan out a course of action with respect to the data, and to enforce its judgments on the will, which is also importuned by the emotions and the appetites.

Three aspects of this psychological theory have a special bearing on the notion of reason inherited by Johnson's age. First, although practical moralists of the Renaissance continually emphasize the conflicts which arise in man's soul—that between reason and emotion, for instance—harmony is the dominating principle in this concept of human nature. Each faculty has its proper function in the service of the whole organism and any conflicts which may arise are due to malfunctions; they are not inherent in the structure itself. Furthermore, the faculty psychology is part of a larger concept of reality, synthetic rather than analytic, which seeks to harmonize and unify everything under the aspect of an elaborate moral and theological hierarchy. Second, despite the fact that the moralists of the Renaissance express their misgivings concerning human nature no less clamorously than moralists of other eras, the faculty psychology is optimistic in its structure— optimistic because man, possessing a divine reason, partakes of Godhead along with the angels, and because this faculty is so conceived as to give man, in theory, a rather large share in shaping his own destiny. Finally, the exponents of this system tend to think of the various faculties of the soul not as operations of some sort of spiritual mechanism but as entities which possessed specific powers. This tendency to think of the faculties as things was encouraged by the Galenic physio-psychology, the humours theory, which grew up alongside of the faculty psychology, and according to which each agency was supposed to be located in some specific organ, the heart, the liver, the brain, and so forth.[1]

---

[1] Some notion of what the faculty psychology involved during its final stages

Now, what are the properties of the Peripatetic reason which functioned within the framework of the faculty psychology? The first thing which strikes one is the remarkable diversity of powers assigned to it. This relative complexity of function persists into the eighteenth century and serves to distinguish the Peripatetic variety from the Lockean. Most important to the moral purposes of Peripatetic reason are a group of powers which tend to free it from complete dependence upon sense data for its knowledge. As we have seen, no matter how much human nature might be ennobled by possessing reason, this divine faculty is by the structure of the tripartite soul forced to receive its information through the mediation of faculties much less perfect, through the agency of the sensitive soul which is possessed by the meanest of brutes.

There are a number of devices by which this hampering restriction could be evaded or compensated for. Most famous of these is the notion of innate ideas, which is certainly not an orthodox Aristotelian concept. Champions of this notion maintained that reason is possessed at birth of certain ideas or principles by which, as the individual develops, he can interpret and evaluate the data of the senses. Another device is to assign to reason intuitive powers which enable it to achieve knowledge not to be accounted for by the operations of ordinary logical processes on the data provided by the senses. Akin to this is the scholastic theory that the reason is somehow able to illuminate sense data and actualize the universals in them. Finally, the restrictions upon this divine faculty could be in some degree compensated for by extensive application of its ordinary capabilities, as when on a foundation of self-evident principles reason is used to erect lofty deductive structures in order to penetrate divine mysteries. The world of the senses is left far behind in this sort of *o altitudo*.

---

can be gained from such compendiums as Pierre La Primaudaye's *The French Academie* (1618) and Burton's *Anatomy of Melancholy*. For a more rigorous contemporary analysis see Bishop Edward Reynolds's *A Treatise of the Passions and the Faculties of the Soul of Man* (1640). A good modern summary is available in Herschel Baker's *The Dignity of Man* (Cambridge, Mass., 1947), pp. 275–292.

These are but some of the devices which, whatever their original purpose, tend to free the Peripatetic concept of reason from bondage to the senses.

That which most incisively distinguishes the older rational faculty is its divine character. It occupies the topmost position in a hierarchy of the soul which is analogous to and at the same time part of a greater, divinely ordained hierarchy which embraces all of creation. As long as reason held this position and was thought to be a faculty proper to God, subordinate faculties— emotion and imagination, for instance—might be praised, but they never could be exalted over reason, as they often were in the latter part of the eighteenth century. Besides assuring the rational faculty pre-eminence, this element of the divine gave to its pronouncements a special authority. They were not merely true, they were binding, for reason is the voice of God. This divine character was largely lost in the intellectual upheavals of the seventeenth century, and with it was lost much of the authority which reason derived from it, a circumstance which had a profound impact on the subsequent history of both psychology and moral thought. In general, eighteenth-century proponents of Peripatetic reason are forced to get along without these divine advantages because they do not accept the scholastic hierarchy of being from which the divinity derived.

These latter-day adherents of the traditional notion of the rational faculty were not numerous, although some of them were influential. Our chief interest is in a group which I will call the moral rationalists. William Wollaston (1659–1724), author of the exceedingly popular *Religion of Nature Delineated* (1722), and Richard Price (1723–1791), who is best remembered by literary scholars as the man who provoked Burke to write his *Reflections on the French Revolution,* are representative of the group. The only other member whose name is familiar to those who are not specialists is a theologian of whom Johnson thought highly,

Samuel Clarke, though perhaps the noted Scottish philosopher, Thomas Reid (1710–1796), should be included among them.[2]

Two moral and psychological convictions characterize this group—their metaphysical speculations do not concern us. By *reason* they mean a faculty which retains some of that power to perceive truth independently of sense data, the power which typified Peripatetic reason, and they differ from some other rationalists and from the majority of their contemporaries in that they consider moral conduct as almost wholly dependent upon the rational faculty. Of course, it was customary for the popular, less systematic moralists to pay tribute to reason as the best guide in moral questions, but as the century wears on, these professions sound increasingly like that lip service which was paid, Sunday in and Sunday out, to the seventeenth of the Thirty-Nine Articles, the one on predestination. Most Englishmen came to think of morality as based on some sense, instinct, or emotion.

The moral rationalist can have such faith in the efficacy of reason because he still believes it to have some of those remarkable powers which were assigned it during the Renaissance. Wollaston, for example, talks very much as the faculty psychologists did a hundred years before:

As there are beings, which have not so much as sense, and others that have no faculty above it; so there may be some, who are indued with reason, but have nothing higher than that. . . . And then if reason be the *uppermost* faculty, it has a right to controll the rest by being *such*.

He dwells at some length on how the senses delude us, but claims that reason will not do so, because

in pure reasoning we use our own ideas for *themselves,* and such as the mind knows them to be, not as representatives of things, that may be falsely exhibited. This *internal* reasoning may indeed be wrongly

[2] For an excellent study of the English ethical rationalists of the eighteenth century by an admirer, see David Daiches Raphael's *Moral Sense* (Oxford, 1947).

applied to *external* things, if we reason about them as being what they are not: but then this is the fault not of reason, but of sense, which reports the case wrong.[3]

Richard Price in even more unmistakable terms rejects the concept upon which the Lockean notion of reason is based, that all our ideas originate either in sensation or from "that notice which the mind takes of its own operations." He believes that the reason has an intuitive access to moral truth independent of sensation:

> Let anyone compare the ideas arising from our powers of sensation, with those arising from our intuition of the natures of things, and enquire which of them his ideas of right and wrong most resemble. On the issue of such a comparison may we safely rest this question.[4]

The reasons why this sort of confidence in the intuitive power of reason is so rare during most of the eighteenth century are too complex to be analyzed here, but it is clear that the decline of the Peripatetic concept was in part due to the rise of the Lockean notion of reason, to which we will now turn.

The only generalization one can make with absolute safety concerning the leaders of the new movement in psychology, beginning, nominally, with Juan Luis Vives (1492–1540) and triumphing with John Locke, is that they were all opposed to some aspect of scholasticism. But the movement as a whole is characterized by the use of empirical and analytical methods to examine the nature of man, in a spirit better described as scientific than as moral or religious. In this new way of thinking, functions which had been regarded as proceeding from faculties of a soul which was in turn neatly fitted into a divinely ordered cosmos, are considered as naturalistic phenomena. Reason, which had been a faculty possessing various powers, becomes an activity of the mind, and, as an activity, it comes to involve only one prin-

---

[3] *The Religion of Nature Delineated* (1738), pp. 51, 53–54.
[4] *A Review of the Principal Questions in Morals,* in L. A. Selby-Bigge's collection, *British Moralists* (Oxford, 1897), II, 124–125.

cipal power of the Peripatetic reason, its logical or discursive function. Gradually all the attributes which enabled the rational faculty to attain knowledge without depending upon the senses were stripped away until only a very restricted concept of reason remained. Joseph Glanvill, in a passage which Johnson quotes in defining *discourse* in the *Dictionary,* remarks on this narrowing of the term: "The act of mind which connects propositions, and deduceth conclusions from them, the schools call *discourse;* and we shall not miscall it, if we name it reason." To put the matter another way, although the proponents of what I have called Lockean reason, continue to use the term *reason,* what they actually intend is *reasoning* or *ratiocination.*

This prosaic conception of the rational faculty predominated in England during Johnson's day. Consider, for example, the writers of the time to whom we usually refer as rationalists. Because they chiefly oppose reason to revelation in matters of religion, I will call them deistic rationalists to distinguish them from the less vociferous moral rationalists who advance reason's claims versus those of irrational faculties in ethics.[5] Matthew Tindal will do as an extreme example of a deistic rationalist. John Leland with some bias declared that Tindal's *Christianity as old as the Creation; or, the Gospel a Republication of the Law of Nature* (1730) endeavors to "subvert the very foundations" of the "Christian scheme" by showing "that external revelation is absolutely needless and useless; that the original law and religion of nature is so perfect that nothing can possibly be added to it by any subsequent external revelation whatsoever." Yet when Tindal finally sets out to describe the exalted faculty which so readily scans the law of nature, it turns out to be much more pedestrian in its operations than one might expect.

All the ideas we have, or can have, are either by sensation or reflec-

---

[5] John Dewey precisely discriminates some of the rationalisms of the eighteenth century in his article "Rationalism" in the *Dictionary of Philosophy and Psychology,* edited by James Mark Baldwin (New York, 1911), II, 415–416.

tion; by the first, we have our ideas of what passes, or exists without; by the second, of what passes or exists within the mind: And in the view, or contemplation of these consists all our knowledge; that being nothing but the perception of the agreement, or disagreement of our ideas.[6]

Indeed, so persistent are the echoes that one is led to suppose that Tindal, when he came to define *reason,* either had before him a copy of *An Essay concerning Human Understanding* open to the seventeenth chapter of the fourth book, or, as many of his contemporaries, had virtually memorized Locke's famous phrases.

Tindal is representative of the whole movement which opposed reason to revelation, for, by and large, this species of rationalist, no matter how much he might exalt man's logical powers, considered reason not a divine faculty or intuition but a mental process, whose operations are based ultimately on the data provided by the senses. It is not surprising that some of the most influential pioneers of deistic rationalism were either close friends of Locke, like Anthony Collins and the third Earl of Shaftesbury, or pretended to be, as did John Toland. This is not the place to speculate as to how it is that deism flourished so, based on such a restricted concept of reason. Hitherto, rational theologians had always depended on the more versatile Peripatetic concept of the faculty; indeed, much of their confidence derived from the remarkable powers they ascribed to it, the same ones the new psychologists discarded. Perhaps the best explanation lies in the great success of the new way of thinking in natural science. In any case, even Samuel Clarke, no deist, and the major figure among eighteenth-century rational theologians who retains something like the traditional concept of reason, denies the existence of innate ideas.[7]

The deistic rationalists are interesting to us chiefly because they were so extreme in their championship of reason's supremacy

---

[6] *Christianity as old as the Creation* (1732), p. 159.
[7] *A Discourse concerning the Being and Attributes of God and the Obligations of Natural Religion* (1749), p. 193.

in matters of religion that they brought down upon their heads the anathemas of the pious; yet in questions of morals they are seldom rationalistic, agreeing generally with their contemporaries that here nonrational aspects of mind are more significant. Tindal, himself, regards as important to morals man's "love for his species; the gratifying of which, in doing acts of benevolence, compassion and good will, produces a pleasure that never satiates." [8] And Shaftesbury, whose pronouncements on revelation, miracles, and prophecies resulted in his being widely regarded as a deist, became the first of a long line of eighteenth-century moralists who developed ethical systems dependent upon emotion or some other nonrational faculty—Bishop Butler, Francis Hutcheson, David Hume, and Adam Smith, for example. Some of these men he influenced profoundly, and to popular sentimental moralists he was a patron saint. The fact that deistic rationalists, the group which is usually referred to when *rationalist* is used in connection with this era, themselves turn away from reason when they seek a basis for moral action, is proof enough of how much the faculty had declined from that pre-eminent position in the moral hierarchy of the soul, which we have seen that it occupied during the Elizabethan period.

Why was reason no longer considered a wholly adequate guide in morals? There is no simple answer to this question, but it is easy enough to see some shortcomings of the Lockean concept as the basis for an ethical system. In the first place, Peripatetic reason was the only faculty of the soul that man shared with God, and its judgments therefore possessed a degree of divine authority; the Lockean concept was the product of a naturalistic analysis of the mind, according to which there was no special justification for regarding one faculty as on a wholly different plane from the others. Secondly, the older faculty, through the medium of innate ideas or intuition, was often regarded as having access to immutable and transcendental truths, so that any moral theory

---

[8] *Christianity as old as the Creation*, p. 17.

based on it was also linked to the fundamental nature of things. We are no longer prone to regard moral knowledge as somehow qualitatively different from other kinds of knowledge, but in Johnson's day it was still customary to do so. The host of new faculties which appeared in the eighteenth century—moral senses, instincts, and emotions—seem to have been intended as touchstones to provide man with what Lockean reason could not provide him, a special knowledge of good and evil not dependent upon the mutable world of sense. Finally, as the century goes on, thinkers become more and more convinced that reason is not potent enough to overcome man's moral inertia.[9] In making ethical behavior depend on pity, sympathy, social love, instinctive benevolence, and the like, moralists of the period were seeking forces strong enough to compel action.

Johnson's position with regard to these questions was not unique but it was heterodox. He seems to accept completely the Lockean concept of the rational faculty, in this agreeing with most of his contemporaries, yet he disagrees with them regarding the functions of reason and concurs with the moral rationalists, considering reason more important to ethical conduct than any other aspect of mind. To put it another way, he retains enough of the traditional humanistic attitude toward the moral function of reason so that it is fair to call him a rationalist in morals, but his epistemology is empirical. Indeed, he puts more drastic restrictions upon the rational faculty than many contemporaries would agree to, especially the deistic species of rationalist, most of whom also were followers of Locke. These rather paradoxical definitions of Johnson's rationalism will seem clearer, as will the motives behind his heterodox ideas, if we consider the two propositions separately: first, that his concept of reason is derived from Locke; and next, in the following chapter, that he tends to apply the faculty much as the moralists of the Renaissance did.

[9] Some notion of how far this tendency had proceeded by the middle of the century can be gained from Section I of David Hume's *An Enquiry concerning the Principles of Morals* (1751).

2

In a thoughtful letter to Mrs. Thrale, Johnson distinguishes the three chief powers of reason as ratiocination, reflection, and judgment.[10] In describing the first of these, which he also calls *reasoning* or *discourse,* Johnson's favorite image is the chain. Ratiocination is a process of concatenation in which a link consists of a simple intuition or a judgment. To proceed "from one truth to another, and connect distant propositions by regular consequences, is the great prerogative of man." The precise meaning and origin of *reflection* are easily determined since John Locke was the first to define it the way Johnson does as "the action of the mind upon itself," as the mind's perception of its own activities.[11] Because both Locke and Watts are cited in the *Dictionary* under *judgment,* two interpretations of Johnson's definition are possible. Locke believed that judgment is exercised when a relation is inferred between two propositions without the benefit of the certain knowledge provided by intuition or ratiocination. Watts, emphasizing the role of will, described judgment as part of the reasoning process. To him, intuitive knowledge of a relation between two propositions did not seem enough. He felt that the assent of judgment is necessary before ratiocination can proceed further; the links in the chain of reasoning, accordingly, are based on judgment rather than intuition, which Watts generally considered as an attribute of spiritual beings, as it is in one of Johnson's definitions. A good case for both meanings of *judgment* could be made on the basis of Johnson's writings and conversation; the most significant consideration here, as with *ratiocination,* and *reflection,* is that the terms which Johnson uses to describe his rationalism are drawn from the British empiricists.

As are Locke and his disciples, Johnson is steadfastly opposed to the theory of innate ideas:

With regard to simple propositions, where the terms are understood,

[10] *Letters,* II, 78–79.
[11] See Locke's *Essay,* II, i, 4, and the *O.E.D.* under *reflection.*

and the whole subject is comprehended at once, there is such an uniformity of sentiment among all human beings, that, for many ages, a very numerous set of notions were supposed to be innate, or necessarily coexistent with the faculty of reason: it being imagined, that universal agreement could proceed only from the invariable dictates of the universal parent.[12]

However "judgment and ratiocination . . . draw their decisions only from experience" [13] and the general consent of mankind arises simply because "human nature is always the same" and truth is unvarying.

Nor is reason capable of knowledge by intuitive perception, for "every mind, however vigorous or abstracted, is necessitated, in its present state of union, to receive its informations, and execute its purposes, by intervention of the body." [14] The definitions given for *intuition* and its derivatives in the *Dictionary* fall into two groups: those referring to the type of immediate knowledge possible to God, "spirits, and angels," which is illustrated from Hooker; and another group dealing with human intuition, which is exemplified from Locke, Glanvill, Dryden, and South. Human intuition is knowledge obtained without the intervention of argument, deduction, or testimony, but, according to the illustration he chooses, such knowledge in men is confined to simple propositions, as it was conceived to be by Locke. Johnson does refer to "those gigantic and stupendous intelligences who *are said* to grasp a system by intuition, and bound forward from one series of conclusions to another, without regular steps through intermediate propositions," [15] but such comments are always carefully qualified, as is this one. As he commonly uses it, *intuition* seems to have for Johnson the same meaning it had for Locke, the perceiving of the relation between simple propositions or ideas, and as such it is the fundamental building block

---

[12] *Works,* IV, 95 (*Adventurer* No. 107).
[13] *Works,* IV, 279 (*Idler* No. 44). See also, for instance, *Works,* III, 216–217 (*Rambler* No. 151), and *Works,* II, 209 (*Rambler* No. 43).
[14] *Works,* III, 216 (*Rambler* No. 151).
[15] *Works,* III, 13 (*Rambler* No. 108), my italics.

upon which all discourse of reason, analytic or synthetic, is based.

Jean H. Hagstrum, who has written two thoughtful and perceptive studies of Johnson's rationalism, would seem to feel that the definition I have proposed for *intuition* is too narrow to fit Johnson's use of the term. In his original essay on the subject, Hagstrum described Johnson as exhibiting contrary empirical and rationalistic impulses. The "empirical faculty" prevails in all instances which do not principally involve morals; in moral matters, reason is the more important.[16] This theory was modified when Hagstrum later revised the essay in order to incorporate it into his valuable *Samuel Johnson's Literary Criticism*. Here the unhistorical notion of a separate empirical faculty is dropped, and, apparently because he now regards Johnson's thought as much more Lockean than he did originally, the dichotomy of empirical and rationalistic impulses is no longer stressed. However, Hagstrum still hesitates to restrict Johnson wholly to the Lockean concept of the rational faculty, as can be seen from this explanation of one of reason's functions, which he reprints from the original essay unchanged:

Reason is an abstracting and generalizing power, of moral importance in detaching the mind from the insistent claims of sense and habit, and of aesthetic importance in guiding the writer to select general and therefore more permanent reality for literary imitation. Here one may see not only the intuitive perception of general truth and nature but also the slower inductive process of generalizing and making abstract those data which were originally concrete.[17]

Only one phrase in this definition contradicts what I have said so far concerning Johnson's rationalism, "the intuitive perception of general truth and nature," but this phrase is crucial, and it will pay us to consider its implications for a moment. As we have seen, a careful examination of Johnson's writings, including the *Dictionary*, reveals only three usages of *intuition:* (a) That im-

---

[16] "The Nature of Dr. Johnson's Rationalism," *ELH*, XVII (1950), 191–205.
[17] *Samuel Johnson's Literary Criticism* (Minneapolis, 1952), p. 15.

mediate perception of truth of which God and the angels are capable. This involves not only knowing but also "seeing" without the intervention of the senses, "mental view," as Johnson calls it. (b) The ability to proceed from particulars to general truth or vice versa without discourse of reason. This power, which resembles the intuitive leap described by William James, is also an attribute of spiritual beings, but Johnson makes it clear that in humans it functions occasionally and then only in remarkable individuals. (c) Lockean intuition, which involves only perception of the certain agreement or disagreement of simple ideas. On the surface, it appears that Hagstrum does not disagree with this classification, for he assures us that when Johnson refers to human intuition he does not mean (a), knowing without the intervention of the senses, but "rather the plainer and less exalted intuition which Locke considered inferior to discursive reason." [18]

But is Locke's concept of intuition adequate for the uses to which Hagstrum says that Johnson puts it? Can it perceive "general truth and nature?" These questions can easily be answered by turning to *An Essay concerning Human Understanding,* for Locke deals with them in most explicit language. Intuitive knowledge is not inferior; it is "the highest of all human certainty." It is certain because it deals with the simplest of mental images. Locke offers the following example: "the mind perceives that an arch of a circle is less than the whole circle, as clearly as it does the idea of a circle; and this, therefore, as has been said, I call intuitive knowledge, which is certain, beyond all doubt, and needs no probation, nor can have any." [19] This sort of intuition cannot help us to certainty regarding "basic moral and natural truth," however, for no matter how simple and plain we may consider this truth to be, by Locke's definition it does not consist of simple ideas but of complex ones, which cannot be perceived intuitively. If, then, as Hagstrum says, "Johnson learned well the

[18] *Samuel Johnson's Literary Criticism,* p. 19.
[19] *Essay,* IV, xvii, 14.

lessons of Locke," it seems improbable that he could believe that intuition is the source of "self-evident, axiomatic propositions" concerning morals.[20]

Locke not only defines the scope of intuition narrowly, he goes further to rule out the very type of proposition to which Hagstrum refers. He does admit that self-evident propositions exist, but he drastically restricts these "maxims," as he calls them, to one particular species. It would be possible, for example, to form a maxim on the basis of the intuition cited above regarding the circle and the arc. We could say that it is self-evident that the whole is greater than the parts, but our justification for doing so would rest firmly on the testimony of ideas derived from the senses, not on any quality of being self-evident possessed by the proposition. This is why Locke remarks that there are an almost infinite number of self-evident propositions, all of them of the same order of complexity as that involving the circle and the arc.[21] Moral propositions Locke specifically excludes:

He would be thought void of common sense, who asked, on the one side, or on the other side went to give a reason, why "it is impossible for the same thing to be, and not to be." . . . But should that most unshaken rule of morality, and foundation of all social virtue, "that one should do as he would be done unto," be proposed to one who never heard it before, but yet is of capacity to understand its meaning, might he not, without any absurdity, ask a reason why.[22]

The reason why Hagstrum is reluctant to think of Johnson as an out and out believer in the Lockean concept of reason seems to be that he fears it would conflict with Johnson's obvious faith in moral absolutes, for, as evidence that Johnson believes reason to be able to perceive general truth intuitively, he offers only two passing allusions from the periodical essays: one to "universal Truths" and another to "abstracted truth." Apparently, Hagstrum is arguing that anyone who believes in absolutes must

---

[20] *Samuel Johnson's Literary Criticism*, p. 19.
[21] *Essay*, IV, vii, 3.
[22] *Essay*, I, iii, 4.

also believe that there exists some way of perceiving them intuitively.[23]

We must postpone consideration of the sources of moral knowledge until a later chapter where it more properly belongs, but it needs no lengthy argument to prove that belief in moral absolutes does not necessarily rule out wholehearted acceptance of the Lockean theory of knowledge. First, as historians of the mind never tire of pointing out, there are paradoxical inconsistencies among the presuppositions of any era. For instance, most of us do not think twice about appealing to modern psychological and sociological principles in one sentence, and to traditional notions of moral responsibility in the next. It would be difficult to catch Johnson in such a radical self-contradiction. Second, joint faith in Locke and absolutes would not set Johnson apart from his contemporaries, for it is obvious to any reader of the literature of mid-eighteenth-century England that belief in moral absolutes is still very much alive, yet by this time acceptance of Locke's epistemology is so widespread that the burden of proof lies on anyone who maintains that a specific individual of the time does not subscribe to it. Finally, John Locke himself declares his belief in moral absolutes,[24] and, although there is some evidence that this faith was a troubled one, there is no reason to doubt its sincerity. We may conclude, then, in the absence of explicit references anywhere in Johnson's works to man's ability to intuit moral and general truths, that Johnson's belief in absolutes does not bar him from accepting restrictions on intuition as readily as he did the other restrictions in the empirical credo. And this is fitting, because, strictly speaking, one ceases to be an empiricist the moment he becomes just a little bit rationalistic in his theory of knowledge.[25]

According to Johnson man has no need of any remarkable

---

[23] *Samuel Johnson's Literary Criticism*, pp. 18–19.

[24] See, for instance, *Essay*, IV, iii, 18–20.

[25] For an ingenious and convincing demonstration of Johnson's empirical habit of thought see W. K. Wimsatt's *Philosophic Words* (New Haven, 1948).

intuitive powers in order to arrive at certain knowledge of most general truths, and therefore no such powers are necessary to explain why men agree concerning these truths. Man can arrive at general truth by systematically subjecting the data of experience to the inductive and deductive processes of the rational faculty. Here, too, I disagree with one aspect of Hagstrum's astute analysis. He seems to suggest that when Johnson relies on deduction he is "rationalistic"—that is, he adheres to what I have called the Peripatetic concept of reason—and that when he uses induction he reveals his empirical tendencies.[26] It is true that the older concept of reason when it flourished during the Middle Ages and the Renaissance was always associated with an excessive dependence upon deduction, but I am not sure that setting up a dichotomy between the two methods of reasoning helps us to understand Johnson any better. "Distinction," as Coleridge remarked, "is not division"—and certainly, it need not imply antithesis.

An examination of the two authors who most influenced Johnson's attitude toward logic, Locke and Isaac Watts, does not show that any antithesis between inductive and deductive methods need be assumed. Locke, to be sure, violently attacks syllogistic reasoning, but he directs his assault principally at formal deduction, a practice that he feels is largely unnecessary because "we reason best and clearest, when we only observe the connexion of the proof, without reducing our thoughts to any rule of syllogism"—which is not to say that we do not deduce. Once it is granted that there is no body of self-evident axioms involving complex ideas upon which it is possible to build up a synthetic account of truth, detached from a firm base in experience, much of the force of Locke's objection diminishes.

Nor does Johnson's admiration for Isaac Watts, who on matters logical is cited even more frequently than his master, necessitate any conflict between the two methods. Watts divides his

[26] "The Nature of Dr. Johnson's Rationalism," *ELH*, XVII (1950), 191–205.

Logick (1725) into four sections dealing with observation, judgment, deduction, and "method." All four are necessary to the attainment of truth. If anything, Watts seems slightly more tolerant of innate ideas than Johnson, but the essential point is that once we admit, as I think we must, that epistemologically both men are thoroughgoing empiricists, the possibility of conflict between the inductive and deductive methods in the thought of either lessens because no one who believes that all knowledge originates in simple sensations is liable to the excesses of the peripatetic logicians.

Finally, Johnson very explicitly describes the basic method by which truth may be attained as a process requiring a balanced collaboration of several intellectual powers. It is after such a process, for instance, that Omar, hero of *Idler* No. 101, models his program of ten years study, and ten years observation followed by a lifetime of combining and comparing. And it is easy enough to find further details:

When a number of distinct images are collected . . . , the fancy is busied in arranging them; and combines them into pleasing pictures with more resemblance to the realities of life as experience advances, and new observations rectify the former.[27]

As we see more, we become possessed of more certainties, and consequently gain more principles of reasoning, and found a wider basis of analogy.[28]

We first discard absurdity and impossibility, then exact greater and greater degrees of probability. . . . Whatever may lull vigilance, or mislead attention, is contemptuously rejected, and every disguise in which errour may be concealed, is carefully observed, til, by degrees, a certain number of incontestable or unsuspected propositions are established, and at last concatenated into arguments, or compacted into systems.[29]

The joint activities of the senses, the imagination, and reason in observing, comparing, and exacting degrees of probability are

---

[27] *Works*, III, 217 (*Rambler* No. 151).
[28] *Journey*, p. 35.
[29] *Works*, III, 217 (*Rambler* No. 151).

inductive; the steps which follow, deductive, and neither phase can stand alone. It was because he took a bearing on what lay at the end, that Johnson was so often able to hold a steady course down the middle of the channel.

Nautical metaphor is rather useful in describing another aspect of Johnson's rationalism that we should note, one in which he diverges not so much from Locke as from Locke's disciples. Johnson feels that man's rational powers can function only within very definite limits, and he constantly points out that the qualities which make reason such a remarkable gift also tempt man to overreach:

> How Heav'n in Scorn of human Arrogance,
> Commits to trivial Chance the Fate of Nations!
> While with incessant Thought laborious Man
> Extends his mighty Schemes of Wealth and Pow'r,
> And tow'rs and triumphs in ideal Greatness;
> Some accidental Gust of Opposition
> Blasts all the Beauties of his new Creation
> O'erturns the Fabrick of presumptuous Reason
> And whelms the swelling Architect beneath it.[30]

However, to assume that Johnson in repeatedly pointing out the limitations of human reason is somehow manifesting irrationalism, is the same as inferring that because a sailor bemoans the deficiencies of the raft on which he is adrift, he would rather swim. This assumption is encouraged by the practice common among modern champions of unreason of setting up a straw man by equating all rationalism with optimism, preferably naive optimism. Actually, though Johnson's rational pessimism seems a proper outgrowth of his individual temperament, it has roots deep in classical tradition. There have always been those who have felt that, no matter how much man may wander guided by its often feeble gleams, reason is a form of light which is all the more to be cherished and preserved if the world about grows darker.

[30] *Poems*, p. 269 (*Irene*, II, iii).

⧅ II ⧆

Reason and Freedom

The paradox of Johnson's rationalism is that despite his acceptance of Locke's restrictions on the rational faculty and despite
his own doubts as to its ability to penetrate very far into the
nature of things, he esteems reason above all other aspects of
mind as a guide in morals. Johnson agrees with most of his
contemporaries regarding the nature of reason, but he dissents
with respect to its functions and sides rather with the older
humanistic tradition and with the moral rationalists of his own
day.

No lengthy demonstration of how much Johnson the moralist
values reason is needed at this point. One cannot read the more
sober essays without noting his persisting esteem for the faculty,
as when he muses on the *carpe diem* theme in *Adventurer* No.
108:

It is likely, that whatever now hinders us from doing that which our
reason and conscience declare necessary to be done, will equally ob-

struct us in times to come. . . . . Good and evil are in real life in-
separably united; habits grow stronger by indulgence; and reason loses
her dignity, in proportion as she has oftener yielded to temptation.
. . . He that now feels a desire to do right, and wishes to regulate his
life according to his reason, is not sure that, at any future time assign-
able, he shall be able to rekindle the same ardour.[1]

This traditional respect for the dignity of reason was evident
enough in the passages cited in regard to the nature of the faculty
in the last chapter, and from one point of view, this entire essay
is concerned with an explication of reason's role in Johnson's
moral thinking.

Our present concern is with why Johnson applies what was
an up-to-date psychological concept, Lockean reason, in the manner of an earlier day. Of course, we could hardly expect him to
sympathize wholly with the men who evolved this new notion
of reason, for when we grant that he and Locke share a strong
faith in the importance of the hard facts of experience, we reach
the end of the essential similarity between the two men. Locke,
his predecessors, and many of his successors look at the mind in
a scientific rather than a moral spirit. Johnson's outlook on the
mind, indeed, on the sum of human experience, is not naturalistic; it is profoundly moral. Thus it might be concluded that
Johnson's ideas often seem to belong to the era before Hobbes
and Locke because he reacted against a novel concept of the purpose of psychology which had been gathering impetus since long
before he was born, a concept which made psychology the servant
of what is, rather than the promoter of what ought to be.

This generalization is true enough, but it does not completely
explain why Johnson is in one sense the last of the Christian
humanists. Notwithstanding the growth of the naturalistic outlook, the eighteenth century is intensely concerned with moral
problems, and it is very easy to find moralists who without looking back to the Renaissance for inspiration manage to be as pro-

[1] *Works*, IV, 101–102.

foundly sincere in their moral convictions as Johnson is. Something else makes Johnson reject the contemporary trend in moral theory—its deterministic nature. The characteristic that distinguishes the moral rationalist most incisively from other moralists of the century is the degree of free will his emphasis on reason confers on man. Johnson seems to look upon adherence to the various moral theories which are based on irrational aspects of mind with the same sort of distaste with which he regards unnecessary vows. The latter, he tells Mrs. Thrale, are a "crime because they resign that life to chance which God has given us to be regulated by reason; and superinduce a kind of fatality, from which it is the great privilege of our Nature to be free." [2] That Johnson clings to the traditional view of reason's function in morals out of more than a reverence for tradition, rather because it guarantees freedom of the will, can be demonstrated from his invariably violent reaction to any notion new or old which tends to limit that freedom.

Consider Johnson's attitude toward the theory of the ruling passion. He does share his age's interest in detecting the man in the child, lamenting, for instance, that there are no records of Sydenham's childhood, because he feels "that the strength of Sydenham's understanding, the accuracy of his discernment, and the ardour of his curiosity, might have been remarked from his infancy by a diligent observer." That small accidents, such as Cowley's chance reading of the *Faerie Queene,* may early determine the whole course of a man's life, Johnson is willing to grant. Sometimes he even depends on "the predominant passion" as a literary device; it is used to characterize both Captator's relatives in *Rambler* No. 198 and the dissembling travelers in the stage coach of *Adventurer* No. 84. But to the notion of the ruling passion as Pope understood it, involving a form of predestination divine in origin and psychological in nature, Johnson is unalterably opposed.

[2] *Letters,* I, 308.

Johnson repudiates the ruling passion in the notes to his translation of Jean Pierre de Crousaz's commentary on Pope's *Essay on Man*,[3] and forty-two years later we find him still repudiating it in the "Life of Pope," where he gives fullest reasons for his opposition. The doctrine is false because "human characters are by no means constant." Furthermore, the objects of this supposititious passion are often of human contrivance, such as money, and "there can be no natural desire of artificial good." Finally, and most important, the

doctrine is in itself pernicious as well as false; its tendency is to produce the belief of a kind of moral predestination or overruling principle which cannot be resisted: he that admits it is prepared to comply with every desire that caprice or opportunity shall excite, and to flatter himself that he submits only to the lawful dominion of Nature in obeying the resistless authority of his "ruling Passion." [4]

To Johnson, a moralist first, the pernicious effects of the theory are more significant than its essential falsity. In the *Commentary* (p. 109) he half-seriously fears

to dwell too long on the resistless Power, and despotick Authority of this Tyrant of the Soul, lest the Reader should, as it is very natural, take the present Inclination however destructive to Society or himself, for the *Ruling Passion,* and forbear to struggle when he despairs to conquer.

It is not enough that men's wills are free; to be moral agents, men must acknowledge this freedom.

The theory of the ruling passion was for the most part a fad; its real importance is as a symptom of a profound change in human attitudes—the growing prestige of nonrational aspects of mind. In popular moral doctrines this change, which, as we have seen, is related to the decline of the faculty psychology and

---

[3] *A Commentary on Mr. Pope's Principles of Morality or Essay on Man* (1739). On p. 109 Johnson suggests that most manifestations of what has been called ruling passion are merely the result of the evocative experiences in childhood mentioned above.

[4] *Lives*, III, 174.

the consequent dethronement of the Peripatetic reason, shows itself in two ways. The determination of right and wrong is in part handed over to moral senses and the like; moral certainty becomes a matter of sensing or feeling something rather than a function of rational conviction. And, second, good actions are more and more ascribed to good emotions instead of to the direction of inferior faculties by reason or to harmony of the faculties. If a man has bad affections, he is a bad man, but if he possesses goodness of heart coupled with a little prudence, he has all that is needed. These notions found their way into every home via the pulpit, the stage, and via a great flood of sentimental and benevolistic literature; and by the end of the century they had become firmly entrenched presuppositions, no more to be doubted by most men than the Copernican hypothesis.

Of course, it can be argued that eighteenth-century England is not unique, that the popular moral consciousness often embraces some irrational doctrine which is likely to be deterministic, whether it be phrenology, the humors theory, or something else. But the experience of Johnson's contemporaries was different in one sense; they had for a while no real alternative. Elizabethan writers rely heavily on the doctrine of the humors—which became popular after the discovery of new manuscripts during the Renaissance had sparked a resurgence of Galenic medicine— yet when the occasion demands that the freedom of the will be asserted, they shift effortlessly over to the spiritual concept of the soul provided by the traditional faculty psychology. The Englishman of 1760 had no such option. Empirical psychology was in its heyday,[5] and what Selby-Bigge calls the "sentimental school" to emphasize their dependence on irrational aspects of mind—Shaftesbury, Hutcheson, Butler, and Hume—dominated ethics.[6] It is odd that with all his erudition Leslie Stephen stresses

[5] For an explanation of the relation of empirical psychology to moral sense, see Raphael's study of Hutcheson in *Moral Sense*, pp. 15–46, or my "Shaftesbury's Moral Sense," *SP*, LII (1955), 17–38.

[6] See the introduction to his *British Moralists*.

the impotence of moral rationalism during this era, and at the same time considers literary sentimentalism, that "mildew which spreads over the surface of literature at this period," as a social, not an intellectual phenomenon.[7] Both sentimentalism and the ascendance of what may be called loosely the school of Shaftesbury are phases of the same general drift toward the nonrational in moral thinking.

Johnson opposed this whole general tendency. No better example of the bitterness of his opposition can be found than the way in which he scoffs at the hoary and respectable idea of natural affection. The notion that all men are endowed with an instinctive affection for their immediate relatives and that those who do not exhibit it are somehow unnatural, was certainly well established in ancient times, and Christians have always been fond of pointing to this instinct as a particularly fortunate instance of Divine Providence, without which the aged and the very young, the race itself, must perish. Johnson, however, belittled this dogma, "Sir, natural affection is nothing: but affection from principle and established duty is sometimes wonderfully strong." [8] An even more extreme example is recalled by Mrs. Piozzi:

Johnson always maintained that no such Attachment naturally subsisted and used to chide me for *fancying* that I loved my Mother. . . . Dr. Johnson said Mr. Thrale was sorry for his only Son's Death, just as a Man frets when he sees his fine new-built House tumble down,— but *no more*. he denied parental Feelings entirely; & said the Cow low'd after the Calf, only because it eased her of the Pain in the Udder: was She constantly kept dry-milked said he, you would hear her low no more.[9]

Mrs. Piozzi, and perhaps, her editor, who contrasts with this statement Johnson's actual comments at the time of Harry Thrale's death, mistake the purpose of these extreme assertions.

[7] *English Thought in the Eighteenth Century* (1881), II, 14, 436.
[8] *Life,* IV, 210.
[9] *Thraliana,* II, 739–740.

There need be no inconsistency, for, despite his unorthodox attitude toward bereavement, Johnson was not denying the depth of that grief which had once so aroused his own compassion. Nor was he wholly serious in denying maternal affection to Mrs. Piozzi; he admitted the existence of such affections frequently enough. What Johnson did balk at is the notion that such affection is *natural* in the sense of *innate,* or, if natural affection does exist from birth, that it is strong enough to be an effective motive to moral action.

Johnson reacted in this manner so puzzling to his friends, because sentimental moralists were using this unquestioned affection or instinct to establish that man is endowed with a whole host of innate affections toward others, culminating finally in a natural affection of universal benevolence. As early as 1672, Richard Cumberland thus concluded a discussion of the intensity of natural affection among humans:

All the *Indications,* deduc'd from this Head, are the *more carefully* to be observ'd, *because* into it is finally to be *resolv'd,* both the reciprocal *Love of Children toward their Parents,* and the *Benevolence of Relations* toward one another, which will, at length, extend itself to a *Love of all Mankind;* when once we come to *know,* from the most authentick Histories . . . that *all Men* are descended from the same *common Parents.*[10]

Later, Shaftesbury felt it safe to define *natural affections* as those "which lead to the Good of the Publick"[11] without even apologizing for extending the meaning, and when he came to revise his *Inquiry* for inclusion in *Characteristicks* he besprinkled the text even more liberally with *natural*. It was with ample precedent, then, that Pope, in his progress from self-love to social, proceeds as if there were no real distinction between familial affections and more comprehensive forms of love:

[10] *A Philosophical Inquiry into the Laws of Nature,* trans. John Maxwell (1727), p. 157 (II, xxviii).

[11] *Characteristicks* (1714), II, 86.

Friend, parent, neighbour, first it will embrace;
His country next; and next all human race.[12]

Some notion of how far this tendency had invaded popular
moral theory by the time Johnson commenced moralist can be
gained from contemporary treatises. Few of them had a more
lasting popularity than the essay written by David Fordyce
(1711–1751) for Dodsley's *Preceptor* (1748).[13] Johnson in his
preface to the *Preceptor* recommends that his young readers
consult Cicero, Grotius, and Puffendorf; and "The Vision of
Theodore," the moral allegory he contributed to the collection,
is rather sternly religious, but it is obvious from the *Preceptor*
that Fordyce was suckled on Shaftesbury and Hutcheson. Natural affections are more violent than other social affections.

The *first* kind [of affections] we approve indeed and delight in, but
we feel still higher Degrees of Approbation and moral Complacence
towards the *last,* and towards all Limitation of the particular Instincts,
by the Principle of *universal Benevolence.* The more Objects the calm
Affections take in, and the worthier these are, their Dignity rises in
Proportion.[14]

Natural affection, then, ultimately is considered inferior to those
affections for which it served as a precedent, and Johnson's scorn
for this instinct is some measure of the annoyance with which
he regarded the spread of affective moral theory.

Something more than the desire to astound or perplex is also

---

[12] *An Essay on Man*, IV, 367–368. The parent came first in the MS version.
Compare *Tom Jones*, VI, i, where Fielding lumps together the pleasures of
"parental and filial affection" with those of "general philanthropy."

[13] It went through one Dublin and seven London editions in its original form;
published separately, it reached its fourth edition in 1769, and was translated
into German. Although it was originally intended for young people, the editors
of the second edition of *Encyclopaedia Britannica* apparently considered it the
best available summary of the subject and adopted it with only slight changes,
and no acknowledgment, as their entry for *Moral Philosophy,* where it occupies
thirty-eight double-column quarto pages. In 1797 the editors of the third edition
felt that it was still useful, though they did make some additions to it.

[14] *The Preceptor* (Dublin, 1765), II, 258. Of course, Johnson would be no
more inclined than Grotius to deny the social nature of man, but the new social
affections went far beyond the *appetitus societatis* of natural law.

involved in Johnson's more broadly heretical convictions that even "pity is not natural to man. Children are always cruel. Savages are always cruel. Pity is acquired and improved by the cultivation of reason." [15] The sister of Sir Joshua Reynolds says concerning his "common assertions that Man was by Nature much more inclined to evil than to good," that "this may appear rather inconsistent with his notions of free will, but I will write the truth and nothing but the truth." [16] The apology is hardly necessary. Johnson is not contradicting himself nor is he temporarily lapsing into Calvinism; he is merely repudiating notions which he thinks will weaken the individual's feeling of moral freedom and the sense of responsibility which attends it.

Of course these notions are untrue:

It is maintained that virtue is natural to man, and that if we would but consult our own hearts we should be virtuous. Now after consulting our own hearts all we can, and with all the helps we have, we find how few of us are virtuous.[17]

But, more important to Johnson, these notions are harmful. The theories which base morality on natural goodness of heart are effectively deterministic, for they pander to human indolence and help produce moral monsters like the one Tim Warner married in *Idler* No. 100. Johnson always "hated a *Feeler*." [18]

The theory of the ruling passion enabled the weak to palliate vice, and sentimental morality led the indolent to substitute feeling for doing, but not all the subverters of the sort of rational freedom which Johnson insisted on were irrationalists. One of his many motives for mistrusting cosmic optimism was the fear that its adherents might repudiate moral responsibility altogether. His most devastating outburst against this pitfall is the satiric

[15] *Life*, I, 437.
[16] *Misc.*, II, 256.
[17] *Life*, III, 352. In reference to Lord Kames's *Sketches of the History of Man*. Compare also the famous passage on the philosopher who lived according to nature, *Rasselas*, ed. R. W. Chapman (Oxford, 1927), pp. 98–99.
[18] *Thraliana*, I, 541.

portrait of Misothea, the prospective bride of Hymenaeus in *Rambler* No. 113; characteristically Johnson is more concerned with the results of believing in determinism than with the truth or falsity of the notion.

Misothea endeavoured to demonstrate the folly of attributing choice and self-direction to any human being. It was not difficult to discover the danger of committing myself for ever to the arms of one who might at any time mistake the dictates of passion, or the calls of appetite, for the decree of fate; or consider cuckoldom as necessary to the general system, as a link in the everlasting chain of successive causes. I therefore told her, that destiny had ordained us to part, and that nothing should have torn me from her but the talons of necessity.[19]

More significant than these reactions against concepts which tend to displace reason from its rightful place in morals are Johnson's positive views on freedom of the will, but there are obstacles to even a tentative summary of this side of his rationalism. For one thing, anyone's attitude toward free will is liable to be determined rather closely by just how effectively he happens to be coping with his environment, and with himself, at the given moment. Johnson is certainly no exception. He may never ascend to the sunny heights of optimism, but his periodic descents into the gulf of dejection do seem to cause a perceptible change in the tone of his writings.

Any precise summary of Johnson's stand on freedom of the will is further complicated by the fact that in addition to fluctuating temperamentally from time to time, he seems to grow progressively more convinced during the period from 1750 to 1780 that men, despite their limitations, can and do accomplish something morally in this world. Manifestly, it seems rather presumptuous to treat the thoughts of a man so intellectually vigorous as Johnson, thoughts expressed over a period of forty or fifty years, as if they were the product of one especially busy afternoon, to make no allowance for that constant flux and

---

[19] *Works*, III, 37.

growth which we all observe, or feel we ought to be able to observe in our own more flaccid minds. Yet we do tend to make this assumption and, justifiably, since Johnson is for the most part remarkably self-consistent over the years. The surface of his thought may have changed, but much of the basic structure developed early and persisted to the end. However, he does grow more optimistic about human nature—though not about the possibility of happiness—perhaps because an increasing tolerance bred in his own bitter struggles leads him to retreat from that rigid ideal of behavior so evident in his earliest moral writings, such as the contributions to Dodsley's *Preceptor.* In 1778, after agreeing with Gibbon that men are seldom just in commercial dealings, Johnson goes on to say,

and really it is wonderful, considering how much attention is necessary for men to take care of themselves, and ward off immediate evils which press upon them, it is wonderful how much they do for others.[20]

And again, about two years before his death,

I look upon myself to be a man very much misunderstood. I am not an uncandid, nor am I a severe man. I sometimes say more than I mean, in jest; and people are apt to believe me serious: however, I am more candid that I was when I was younger. As I know more of mankind, I expect less of them, and am ready now to call a man *a good man,* upon easier terms than I was formerly.[21]

A final difficulty in determining how Johnson felt about free will is part of the general problem which confronts anyone who seeks to interpret him as a moralist; how much of what he is saying on a particular occasion does he say because it is what he feels his audience *ought* to hear? This is not to accuse him of deviousness; however, for therapeutic purposes he often shifts his emphasis to suit the audience and the occasion, and he is always intensely aware of both. The youthful readers of the

[20] *Life,* III, 236.
[21] *Life,* IV, 239.

Preceptor are worlds away from the society at Streatham, and there is a vast difference between an evening with the Club and Sunday morning in the pulpit at Ashbourne. Note, for instance, how much the tone of the *Ramblers* changes around Christmas and Easter. To be sure, these were occasions when he himself was given to somber meditation, but the *Ramblers* become grave largely because he feels that during these seasons his readers should also meditate on how pitifully weak man is and how little he can accomplish on his own. Were an estimate of man's freedom of choice based on these essays, the answer would be that he has little or none. Neither the fluctuations of Johnson's frame of mind, nor his increasing tendency to regard men favorably, nor the fact that he is perpetually the moralist preclude finding out how much real freedom he is willing to grant man, but they must always be kept in mind while the evidence is being weighed.

For our purposes, the restraints upon freedom of choice and upon the accomplishment of what is chosen can be simplified to three: the limitations proper to the individual himself, accidents external to the individual, and the possibility that both the individual and his environment are subject to some sort of overriding determinism. Let us consider what Johnson says about each in turn. He habitually defines individual limitations in terms of appetite and passion and the drives which they produce in conjunction with imagination, and, although Johnson absolutely rejects any notion, such as the ruling passion, which implies that these irrational elements are inherently deterministic, he certainly is not sanguine about the possibility of men as a whole bringing these elements into harmony with reason. The sage who so impressed Rasselas upon his first visit to the school of declamation erred not because he believed that men should strive to keep their passions harmoniously subordinate, but because he was fool enough to maintain that absolute dominance by reason "was in every one's power"—and desirable. Hymenaeus is wise in rejecting Misothea who may seek to transfer the responsibility for her own failings to some external necessity. The chances are that even if she herself definitely accepts the responsibility, "the dictates of passion or the calls of appetite" may still determine her behavior, but unless she accepts it there is no hope at all. The limited rationalism I have tried to define conversely defines Johnson's attitude on the nonrational aspects of mind. In practice they are generally dominant; reason can be ascendant, however, and the individual must act as if it will be, even though the best he is likely to achieve is a compromise or uneasy truce, not victory.

If Johnson grants a limited amount of rational choice to men, what is it that chiefly determines whether or not a given choice will result in some specific good? His answer is simple enough—chance; with regard to that, "men will always find reasons for confidence or distrust, according to their different tempers or inclinations." [22] As Johnson's temper varies or his intent changes, so to some extent does the degree of importance which he assigns chance in human affairs; yet he is never very optimistic. A passage from *Adventurer* No. 69 is typical:

We are all ready to confess, that belief ought to be proportioned to evidence or probability: let any man, therefore, compare the number of those who have been thus favoured by fortune, and of those who have failed of their expectations, and he will easily determine, with what justness he has registered himself in the lucky catalogue. [23]

Even though bad luck is a principal cause of failure, success cannot be considered as victory over chance, because here, too, accident has its part.

In every great performance, perhaps in every great character, part is the gift of nature, part the contribution of accident, and part, very often not the greatest part, the effect of voluntary election, and regular design. [24]

[22] *Works,* IV, 48 (*Adventurer* No. 69).
[23] *Works,* IV, 49.
[24] *Works,* VI, 439 (King of Prussia).

The authority of chance is not, to be sure, uniformly effective. Johnson, following classical moralists, usually emphasizes the force of circumstance to point out the vanity of seeking worldly happiness and success. Moral accomplishment is much less subject to this tyranny. In his more somber moments, though, he abandons all human achievement to the government of chance.[25] Yet, man must not submit to this tyranny, inexorable as it may be, for if he does so he becomes as morally impotent as the most devout believer in necessity.[26] Again, the ethical results of a notion seem more important to Johnson than its truth or falsity.

How, then, can the individual, his freedom hobbled by both his own nature and by external circumstance, maintain the necessary faith in his potential for rational accomplishment? In one of his answers to this question Johnson comes closer than anywhere else to the third type of restraint on human freedom, an overriding determinism. Yet, there is a qualitative difference which sharply distinguishes his views from those of the fatalists whom he abhorred.

In this state of universal uncertainty, where a thousand dangers hover about us, and none can tell whether the good that he pursues is not evil in disguise, or whether the next step will lead him to safety or destruction, nothing can afford any rational tranquility, but the conviction that, however we amuse ourselves with unideal sounds, nothing in reality is governed by chance, but that the universe is under the perpetual superintendence of Him who created it; that our being is in the hands of omnipotent Goodness, by whom what appears casual to us, is directed for ends ultimately kind and merciful.[27]

What distinguishes Johnson from the cosmic optimist, pious and otherwise, is his conviction that events *must always* appear "casual to us," in our present state. For practical purposes man must consider himself bound only by his own nature and by circumstance, since there is no real difference between the reign

---

[25] *Rambler* No. 184, for instance, was written in this mood.
[26] See, for example, *Rambler* No. 29, *Adventurer* No. 69, and *Life,* IV, 122–123.
[27] *Works,* III, 361–362 (*Rambler* No. 184).

of accident and a determinism whose workings are completely inscrutable.

Accordingly, the pessimistic Johnson's frequent and vehement assertions of the will's freedom in reply to Boswell's taunting questions represent neither bravado nor arrogant dogmatism. Elsewhere he defines and limits this freedom explicitly enough. It is significant that the limitations result from human weakness and the force of circumstance, for these two hindrances always leave the possibility of some responsible accomplishment, some freedom of movement; whereas, binding human nature fast in fate, leaves none.

2

It can be objected that so far I have carefully avoided mentioning one of Johnson's works which contradicts what has just been said. Since the objection is justified, it will pay to examine in some detail the implications of *The Vanity of Human Wishes*. We cannot expect to resolve many of the perplexities which are woven into the fabric of the poem, but such an examination should throw more light on Johnson's concept of freedom of the will. Certainly, whatever the outcome of the recent efforts to modify the traditional interpretation of *Rasselas*,[28] it is only half true that the book is a *Vanity of Human Wishes* in prose. Because both the poem and the tale are pessimistic, critics tend to equate them in a perfunctory way without staying to mark that the pessimisms differ in kind. However, since profoundly divergent moral implications are involved, we can be sure that Johnson would be sensitive to the difference between depicting the defeat of man's loftiest endeavors by an implacable fate in the *Vanity* and saying in *Rasselas* that the individual cannot achieve personal happiness because he is the victim of his own foibles and

---

[28] See, for example, Clarence R. Tracy, "Democritus Arise!, A Study of Dr. Johnson's Humor," *Yale Review*, XXXIX, 294–310. Alvin Whitley, "The Comedy of Rasselas," *ELH*, XXIII (March 1956), 48–70.

of chance. The two works are so different in essence that the best way to demonstrate the fatalism of the poem is to contrast it to *Rasselas*.

Johnson gives us no opportunity to mistake the subject of *Rasselas,* for the first volume is in the form of an extended statement that personal happiness is illusory, followed by a number of variations on the theme—variations which all end on the same note. At first, Rasselas believes himself the only unhappy man in the happy valley, but he finds out that Imlac, the wisest inhabitant, is only "less unhappy" than himself and that "the rest, whose minds have no impression but of the present moment, are either corroded by malignant passions, or sit stupid in the gloom of perpetual vacancy." Rasselas goes forth into the world in the belief that "surely happiness is somewhere to be found." He and his sister "enter Cairo, and find every man happy," but this happiness soon turns out to be as false as that in the valley. "The prince finds a wise and happy man" who when confronted with personal misfortune proves to be neither. And he examines in turn the specious happinesses "of pastoral life," prosperity, solitude, "of a life led according to nature," and "of high stations." In every instance, the lesson of the happy valley is repeated.

The credulity of Rasselas can hardly be sustained much longer, nor need it be, and in the second volume Johnson turns away from this repetitious structure to inquire into the grounds of the maxim which he has inculcated by repetition, that "happiness is never to be found." One of the reasons why this is true has already been suggested by the continual references to uncertainty Johnson has spread through the first volume. The chance illness and death of the philosopher's daughter destroys his fancied independence of external things. Because "the favour of the great is uncertain," the rich man lives in constant fear, as does the Bassa himself. All travel "under the conduct of chance." Even the choice of life which Rasselas thinks to be crucial, is not. Imlac points out that the causes of good and evil ... are so various and uncertain, so often entangled with each other, so diversified by various relations, and so much subject to accidents which cannot be foreseen, that he who would fix his condition upon incontestable reasons of preference, must live and die inquiring and deliberating.[29]

More radical and pervasive causes of human unhappiness are explored in the second volume. Johnson seeks to explain why the "happy" valley mirrors the world, despite the fact that the valley's inhabitants are in a large degree exempt from the whims of chance. Although there is little solace in the knowledge, Rasselas discovers that in one very ironic sense his original hypothesis that "man has surely some latent sense for which this place affords no gratification, or he has some desires distinct from sense which must be satisfied before he can be happy,"[30] is valid. "This place," he learns, is not the valley, but the world, and while it is true that desire must be satisfied before man can be happy, it also follows that because his imagination will in its incessant hunger fashion new objects of desire, man can never be happy.

This is a simplified statement of what is actually a subtle and complex response to the problem of man's perpetual discontent, a response which has its positive side.[31] But only two features of this response are relevant to the question at issue here: Johnson feels that man is for the most part self-thwarted, and because the inquiry is confined to happiness, the obvious moral is not drawn—in *Rasselas,* at least, nothing is concluded. With respect to the first of these two points, it could be argued that the workings of fate are manifested in the nature of man, that each man is just as inexorably doomed by his own nature as he ever could be by any force from without. On the other hand, the only thing which is determined is that he shall be unhappy; there the inevitability

[29] *Rasselas,* p. 79.
[30] *Rasselas,* p. 15.
[31] This response and the positive implications it involves with respect to development of the individual are examined perceptively in W. J. Bate's *The Achievement of Samuel Johnson* (New York, 1955).

ends. Perhaps Johnson's arguments sound so much less deterministic than those of moralists who depict man in bondage to specific
passions because he constantly stresses the part played by that
most free-ranging and protean of all the faculties, the imagination.

The absence of a moralizing conclusion is also relevant to
Johnson's attitude toward free will. It is true that the young
travelers finally come to realize what Imlac had known all along,
that a search for the choice of life which will make them most
happy is not only futile but dangerous too, because it wastes time.
This lesson is provided near the end of their journey by the old
man who has learned from the vicissitudes of this world to turn
his thoughts to the next. But even when Nekayah, in the penulti-
mate chapter, after an appropriate visit to some tombs and a
discourse on the soul by Imlac, declares that she hopes "hereafter to think only on the choice of eternity," we are more struck
by the opportunity Johnson missed to dwell on the *de contemptu
mundi* theme than by his passing reference to it. The reader is
left with no feeling that Rasselas was written for some ulterior
moral purpose, as so many tales of this nature are. It deals with
the nature of man and his pursuit of happiness in an uncertain
world. These are subject enough, as Johnson confirms by return-
ing to them in the final chapter.

Although he denies that man can win happiness, Johnson, by
confining himself in *Rasselas* to this one impossibility, still leaves
man some freedom to act; in *The Vanity of Human Wishes* he
leaves him almost none. It is better to be the "vassal," the skulk-
ing "hind," "the needy traveller, serene and gay," than to strive
greatly for any goal—and the substitution of Christian resignation
for this lowly apathy in the concluding lines of the poem does
little to relieve this impression. Unlike the various exemplars
whom Rasselas meets along the way, the characters of *The
Vanity of Human Wishes* are not seeking mere happiness or

content; they are great men who have gone beyond the pursuit of a pleasant existence to accept the challenges of the imagination, and so are representative of the sum of human achievements good and bad. Johnson had reason to admire some of his characters— Laud, Lydiat, Hyde, and Galileo—; others, such as Swift and Harley, he sometimes contemned, but their merits are not important to the theme of the poem, which is the defeat of the spirit of man in "the clouded mazes of fate," a theme which is most powerfully expressed in the magnificent lines on Charles the Twelfth.

Because this fatalism is not typical of Johnson, it is natural to assume that it did not originate with him but with Juvenal. Quite the opposite is the case. As Francis G. Schoff has demonstrated, the imitation is far more pessimistic than the original.[32] Professor Schoff bases his conclusions on the fact that Juvenal seems to allot most of the blame for human failure to human folly, while Johnson emphasizes the responsibility of external forces. Our concern is not so much that the forces which cause the individual man to fail are often external to him—this notion is common to all of Johnson's reflections on the subject—but that in *The Vanity of Human Wishes* these forces seem to be due to necessity rather than accident and that even when he does refer to the concept of fortune or chance he seems to follow medieval and classical practice in emphasizing inevitability instead of fortuitousness.

The pronounced fatalistic tendency of the poem is obvious even in its language and imagery. In Juvenal's satire *fatum* is used but three times, *fortuna* and its derivatives, but five, and in the last verses we learn that *nos te, nos facimus, Fortuna, deam*

---

[32] "Johnson on Juvenal," *N&Q*, CXCVIII (1953), 293–296. Both Henry Gifford, in *"The Vanity of Human Wishes,"* *RES*, VI (1955), 157–165, and Mary Lascelles, in "Johnson and Juvenal," printed in *New Light on Dr. Johnson* (New Haven, 1959), pp. 35–55, while not stressing the fatalistic tone of Johnson's poem, do make it very clear that his chief intent is to present a tragic view of life, whereas Juvenal's intent is largely satirical.

caeloque locamus. In *The Vanity of Human Wishes, fate* and *fatal* occur eleven times and it is obvious that Johnson is making a play on his definition of *fatal* as "proceeding by destiny; inevitable, necessary," in passages such as this,

> Fate wings with ev'ry wish th'afflictive dart,
> Each gift of nature, and each grace of art,
> With fatal heat impetuous courage glows,
> With fatal sweetness elocution flows.

[lines 15–18]

Doom is another favorite word, and, as Professor Schoff points out, fortune is used in such a way as to suggest the medieval wheel of fortune:

> Delusive Fortune hears th'incessant call,
> They mount, they shine, evaporate, and fall.

[lines 75–76]

The image of falling, recurrent in both poems offers a good example of how Johnson transformed what is usually in the original a rather simple image with few overtones, into a figure more richly suggestive and more suitable to the fatalistic tone of his imitation.[33] Twice in *The Vanity of Human Wishes* the fall or decline is into the "gulphs of fate." What Johnson intended by this image can be inferred from the definitions he gives for *gulf* in the *Dictionary* and the illustrations of usage which had already been chosen when he wrote the poem. Johnson's second definition, "an abyss; unmeasurable depth," is the most relevant one. Two of the applicable illustrations refer to the *Aeneid* and picture specifically the mouth of hell; it is likely the third, "fiery gulf," from *Coriolanus,* does also. Johnson thought of a gulf, then in Spenser's terms, as "the yawning gulf of deep Avernus' hole" or it brought to mind the spectacular fall of the river Velino, near Terni, as described by Addison in the other illustration, the seem-

---

[33] Gifford sees the far greater number of images of falling and sinking in the imitation as proof that it is more grave and exhibits more visionary depth than does the original.

ingly bottomless "gulf through which Virgil's Alecto shoots herself into hell." This description suggests still a third image from the poem,

> Must helpless man, in ignorance sedate,
> Roll darkling down the torrent of his fate? [34]
>
> [lines 345–346]

Two of Johnson's other definitions of *gulf* have some pertinence; it is "a sucking eddy," "any thing insatiable." Juvenal made his point with the frightful or ironic falls of individuals; nowhere does he suggest anything so vast and awesome, so inevitably all-devouring as the image we have been discussing. And fortunate are those who decline "unclouded in the gulphs of fate."

The uniquely fatalistic tone of *The Vanity of Human Wishes* is as difficult to explain as it is to ignore. A partial explanation—and this is best we can expect—is to be found in two of the variables I have described as obstacles to any neat summary of Johnson's attitude toward freedom: the tendency of his attitude toward free will to fluctuate along with Johnson's various moods, and also according to the ultimate purpose which Johnson has in mind at the moment. Professor Clifford points out that

during the autumn of 1748 Johnson was actually in a somber mood. . . . He was still plagued by financial worries, illness, and his old constitutional lethargy. . . . But the chief cause of his low spirits was undoubtedly domestic. At home there was little or nothing to cheer him when he came downstairs after hours of drudgery in the garret. Tetty's health was poor, her temper uncertain, her petty demands increasing. She was no happy wife to calm his jaded nerves or talk him out of his melancholy. Marriage, he was gradually finding out, had many pains.[35]

Thus, although we might, had we the incentive we have here, find many periods when Johnson had even more reason to be

---

[34] 1755. The original version suggests a less precipitous descent: "Swim darkling down the current of his fate."

[35] *Young Sam Johnson* (New York, 1955), p. 310.

pessimistic; there is little doubt that he wrote *The Vanity of Human Wishes* in a more than ordinarily gloomy era of his life.

There is some proof that the fatalism is the product of a transient mood in the fact that five years later Johnson interpreted the closing lines of Juvenal's tenth satire in a spirit entirely different from that of *The Vanity of Human Wishes.* In *Adventurer* No. 111, Johnson says "that the satirist advised rightly, when he directed us to resign ourselves to the hands of Heaven," but he limits resignation to those things which can only be granted by heaven, in this instance, "the dignity of high birth and long extraction." Here the will of heaven, though it may seem harsh at first, is actually beneficent, because only those of humble birth can feel the full satisfaction of achievement. Thus, the same lines which he interpreted in 1748 as counseling passive resignation ironically come to serve in 1754 as a gloss on one of Johnson's finest statements of the necessity for striving:

To strive with difficulties, and to conquer them, is the highest human felicity; the next is, to strive, and deserve to conquer: but he whose life has passed without a contest, and who can boast neither success nor merit, can survey himself only as a useless filler of existence; and if he is content with his own character, must owe his satisfaction to insensibility.[36]

That Johnson was dejected when he wrote the poem also seems to be confirmed by "The Vision of Theodore" (1748), which is very pessimistic in tone and suggests that there is little hope that the individual will accomplish anything morally by means of his reason alone. But the strongly didactic bent of the "Vision" is probably more significant in explaining why both it and *The Vanity of Human Wishes* are even less optimistic than so much of what Johnson wrote and said. The moral which he refrained from drawing in *Rasselas* is enforced in *The Vanity of Human Wishes.* We cannot read the peroration to the poem without sensing that one of the chief purposes of the whole effort has

[36] *Works,* IV, 108–109. The lines he cites from Satire X are 347–349.

been to promote virtue and religion by instilling contempt for the world.

In *The Vanity of Human Wishes,* as in "The Vision of Theodore," Johnson is exercising the moralist's license to overstate. He certainly believes that in ordinary life

to walk with circumspection and steadiness in the right path, at an equal distance between the extremes of errour, ought to be the constant endeavour of every reasonable being.[37]

But the problem is more complicated for the moralist, whose task it is to keep others walking at an equal distance from each extreme, for if he decides that his charges have veered off course in one direction, he has no choice but to veer in the other. In order to achieve the immediate goal of bringing them back on center, he himself must violate the mean; with respect to this goal, truth becomes duplex and the aspect which is to be emphasized depends on the conditions of the moment. Johnson wrote the best annotation on *The Vanity of Human Wishes:*

Some have endeavoured to engage us in the contemplation of the evils of life for a very wise and good end. They have proposed, by laying before us the uncertainty of prosperity, the vanity of pleasure, and the inquietudes of power, the difficult attainment of most earthly blessings, and the short duration of them all, to divert our thoughts from the glittering follies and tempting delusions that surround us, to an inquiry after more certain and permanent felicity not subject to be interrupted by sudden vicissitudes, or impaired by the malice of the revengeful, the caprice of the inconstant, or the envy of the ambitious.[38]

Neither moral expediency nor personal sorrows may seem adequate to explain why *The Vanity of Human Wishes* is so deterministic, but, at least, if they are not, it is because we realize to what extent the determinism is anomalous. Johnson's rationalism surely has an opposite intent. Although he draws his concept

[37] *Works,* II, 123 (*Rambler* No. 25).
[38] *Works,* IX, 331 (Sermon V). For Johnson's discussion of this sort of moralizing see *Rambler* No. 29, *Adventurer* No. 108.

of reason from Locke, he applies the concept after the fashion of an earlier day, and demands that the individual accept freedom unequivocally and with it, responsibility. Johnson's own actions provide more evidence of this conviction, because his life is an excellent illustration of the difference between pessimism and fatalism. Johnson did suffer the anguish and depression of melancholy, and he was capable of great patience and forbearance when he was confronted with adversity, but he never ceased to struggle.

ℰ III ℨ

The Nature of Johnson's Altruism

The chief difficulty with regard to the question which is now to be asked of Johnson—"what is the moral life?"—is that he gives so many answers. Somehow out of a welter of Johnsonian precepts we must select for discussion those which are fundamental, and we must do so without imposing any order or pattern on Johnson's notions which is not actually inherent in them. The task of winnowing out what is most important is simplified in one respect because Johnson devotes much of his energy to banishing folly rather than to preventing knavery. Many of his familiar subjects, self-knowledge, the art of bearing calamities, the need for perseverance, and so forth, are either merely instrumental to virtuous behavior or they relate to the immediate goal of individual happiness. Since the man who is rational in the pursuit of his personal happiness is most likely to see that the ultimate happiness lies in virtue, and since the fool can be moral only by accident, every moralist must inculcate prudence. It is also true that because folly is universal and perpetual, the prudential part of Johnson's moralizing is enduringly pertinent. On the other hand, if to simplify our task something must be left out, it seems most appropriate that this part be. This familiar area has been thoroughly studied,[1] and here much of Johnson's effectiveness derives from the trenchant and sincere fashion in which he urges traditional wisdom. For the most part it is the expression rather than the thought which is distinctively Johnsonian. Accordingly, we will modify our query to read, "What must the prudent man do to act rightly?" with the understanding that we do so without any intent to beg the question of whether the ultimate purpose of all moral action may not be the individual's happiness, development, or self-realization—these possibilities can be taken later when we consider the "why?" rather than the "what?" of Johnson's moral notions.

By limiting discussion of Johnson's concept of the moral life in this way we are making use of his own distinction of goodness into "soberness, righteousness, and godliness," which involve respectively the individual's relationship to himself, to other men, and to God.[2] The classification is traditional, deriving ultimately from Paul's words to Titus, which were adopted in the *Book of Common Prayer*. It was especially familiar in eighteenth-century England because that most influential of all treatises of popular morality, *The Whole Duty of Man,* is divided in such a manner. If prudence is passed over, soberness is in effect eliminated from our discussion, for Johnson is little interested in those other aspects of the individual's relationship to himself with which religious moralists are preoccupied. Under this heading the author of *The Whole Duty,* for instance, speaks mostly of

---

[1] Walter Jackson Bate's *The Achievement of Samuel Johnson,* for instance, should for a long time remain the definitive study of Johnson as a moral psychologist.

[2] *Works,* IV, 412 (*Idler* No. 89). He also uses this classification in the *Prayers and Meditations, Misc.,* I, 61.

temperance, on which Johnson seldom dwells, and chastity, which he almost never discusses.

With soberness excluded, and godliness deferred until we consider the relation of Johnson's moral notions to his religious beliefs, our concern is with his concept of righteousness, which involves the conduct of the individual toward others. We shall see that to Johnson righteousness generally means altruism, but this latter term is too broad to be useful. More specific terms, such as *benevolist,* automatically bring to mind contemporaries with whom he strongly disagrees. The problem, therefore, is to formulate a definition which justly applies to Johnson's altruism and distinguishes it from other species. Such a definition will necessarily be extensive, for Johnson has strong convictions regarding conduct toward others, convictions dealing with everything from domestic relations to the individual's relation with "the great community of mankind." Fortunately, most of these tenets derive logically from a limited number of underlying principles.

One thing which simplifies the discussion is the fact that the same fundamentally humane spirit with which readers of Boswell's *Life* are familiar informs some of Johnson's earliest writing. We need only describe his altruism, not trace its development. In one of Johnson's earliest works, *Irene,* Mahomet charms the heroine "with the thought of blessing human kind," and Aspasia's

> Bosom feels, enkindled from the Sky,
> The lambent Flames of mild Benevolence,
> Untouch'd by fierce Ambition's raging Fires.[3]

And the same impulse which in 1735 made him attack the Jesuits for not showing "universal and unbounded charity and benevolence" toward the natives of Abyssinia is evident nine years later in the *Life of Savage* where the "benevolence," the "humanity,"

---

[3] *Poems,* p. 293 (*Irene,* III, viii, 108–110).

"the tenderness that is excited by pity, and all the zeal which is kindled by generosity" as they are manifested in the hero's benefactors are repeatedly contrasted with the inhuman malignity of his supposed mother.

The first thing which must be done in describing what Johnson means by benevolence, or beneficence, as he was more likely to term it, is to distinguish it from the sentimentalism that was so much in vogue during his lifetime. It is natural enough to associate the two terms because they are both involved in that great popular moral ideal of Johnson's day, "goodness of heart" or "good nature." For instance, few of Sir John Hawkins's contemporaries would agree with his strictures on Fielding:

His morality, in respect that it resolves virtue into good affections, in contradiction to moral obligation and a sense of duty, is that of Lord Shaftesbury vulgarised, and is a system of excellent use in palliating the vices most injurious to society. He was the inventor of that cant-phrase, goodness of heart, which is everyday used as a substitute for probity, and means little more than the virtue of a horse or dog.[4]

On the other hand, most of them would agree with Arthur Murphy's retort, that Hawkins

should have known that kind affections are the essence of virtue; they are the will of God implanted in our nature, to aid and strengthen moral obligation; they incite to action; a sense of benevolence is no less necessary than a sense of duty.[5]

Even such diverse individuals as the sentimental Laurence Sterne and that strenuous humanitarian, Jonas Hanway, whose views on tea drinking annoyed Johnson, speak in the same terms, though their meanings are worlds apart. In 1759 Adam Smith remarked that "philosophers have, of late years, considered chiefly the tendency of the affections," and he might have added that

---

[4] *Life of Johnson* (1787), p. 215.
[5] "An Essay on Johnson's Life and Genius," *Misc.,* I, 441. Compare Boswell's praise of Fielding for his tendency to cherish the "benevolent and generous affections," *Life,* II, 49.

they also had made ethics chiefly a matter of good will toward others, or benevolence. While Johnson conforms in accepting altruism as the principle which should govern all aspects of the individual's conduct toward others, he rejects every manifestation of the ethics of sentiment.

Johnson's attitude regarding sentimentalists, or feelers, as he preferred to call them, is well known. There is, for instance, the portrait of Mrs. Tim Warner, nee Gentle, in *Idler* No. 100, who

daily exercises her benevolence by pitying every misfortune that happens to every family within her circle of notice; she is in hourly terrours lest one should catch cold in the rain, and another be frighted by the high wind. Her charity she shows by lamenting that so many poor wretches should languish in the streets, and by wondering what the great can think on that they do so little good with such large estates.[6]

Johnson's chief objection to such people is that they feel instead of doing. When Boswell apologized "for not feeling for others as sensibly as many say they do," Johnson replied, "Sir, don't be duped by them any more. You will find these very feeling people are not very ready to do you good. They *pay* you by *feeling*." [7]

Richard Cumberland (1632–1718), who was the first to construct a systematic basis for the ethics of altruism, saw this danger and warned his readers against it:

The Reader is to observe, that I no where understand by the Name of *Benevolence,* that languid and lifeless Volition of theirs, which *effects nothing* of what they are said to desire; but that only, by force whereof we *execute,* as speedily and thorowly as we are able, what we heartily desire.[8]

The weakness of this precaution lies in the fact that *benevolence* refers merely to willing, not acting. One characteristic which sets Johnson apart from Cumberland and from moralists such as

---

[6] *Works*, IV, 442.
[7] *Life*, II, 95.
[8] *The Laws of Nature*, pp. 41–42.

Hutcheson and Adam Smith is that he never uses *benevolence* loosely; he never intends more by it than the definition he gives in the *Dictionary*, "disposition to do good." Wherever possible he uses *beneficence*, "the practice of doing good"—the difference is that between *volo* and *facio*. This distinction seems clear enough to us, yet it was not always clear in the minds of his contemporaries.

The trouble with feelers is not simply that they are so involved with their own emotions that they have no intention of relieving those with whom they commiserate; Johnson maintains that even if they did intend to do so, unaided emotion would not be sufficiently powerful to make them act. Man's emotions are certainly the mainspring of his actions, but Johnson has no faith whatsoever in the power of the other-regarding, good affections to triumph alone over excessive self-love, or affections positively evil, such as hate and envy.

This conviction undercuts all the serious moralists of the day who based their hopes for a better world upon good affections, and it raises the question of just what part Johnson does believe the emotions play in a beneficent action. To some, his attitude seemed so unorthodox that they thought he denied any role to good emotions. Hester Mulso, later Mrs. Chapone, in a letter to Elizabeth Carter thus commented on a visit Johnson made to her home in 1753.

I had the assurance to dispute with him on the subject of human malignity, and wondered to hear a man who by his actions shews so much benevolence, maintain that the human heart is naturally malevolent, and that all the benevolence we see in the few who are good, is acquired by reason and religion.[9]

No doubt this optimistic young disciple of Richardson provoked Johnson to make his point more strongly than he might have on some occasions, and we do know he became more tolerant of human failing as he grew older, yet twenty-three years later

[9] *Works* (4 vols.; 1807), I, 73.

when Boswell lamented his own lack of sympathy with the Thrales in their sorrow over the death of Harry, but declared that he would do all in his power to relieve them, Johnson replied,

Sir, it is an affectation to pretend to feel the distress of others, as much as they do themselves. It is equally so, as if one should pretend to feel as much pain while a friend's leg is cutting off, as he does. No, Sir; you have expressed the rational and just nature of sympathy. I would have gone to the extremity of the earth to have preserved this boy.[10]

Nor does feeling, even strong feeling, necessarily imply the will to relieve. "We may have uneasy sensations from seeing a creature in distress, without pity; for we have not pity unless we wish to relieve them." [11] Reason is necessary, too; Johnson would have man "meditate on the excellence of charity, and improve those seeds of benevolence, which are implanted in every mind, but which will not produce fruit, without care and cultivation." [12] And to reason must be added piety, which is why hospitals and homes for foundlings were unknown among the ancients.

Charity, or tenderness for the poor, which is now justly considered, by a great part of mankind, as inseparable from piety, and in which almost all the goodness of the present age consists, is, I think, known only to those who enjoy, either immediately or by transmission, the light of revelation.[13]

To sum it up, Johnson believes that beneficent actions result from an affection, weak in itself, which is improved by the instructions of reason and the admonition of religion.

If social love is naturally so weak and self-love so strong, might it not be possible that our "altruistic" actions derive wholly from the latter? This is the tack Mandeville takes in explaining them:

[10] *Life*, II, 469.
[11] *Life*, I, 437.
[12] *Works*, IX, 322 (Sermon IV).
[13] *Works*, IV, 160.

Charity is that Virtue by which part of that sincere Love we have for our selves is transferr'd pure and unmix'd to others, . . . This Virtue is often counterfeited by a Passion of ours, call'd *Pity* or *Compassion,* which consists in a Fellow-feeling and Condolence for the Misfortunes and Calamities of others: all Mankind are more or less affected with it; but the weakest Minds generally the most. It is raised in us, when the Sufferings and Misery of other Creatures make so forcible an Impression upon us, as to make us uneasy.[14]

Johnson seems to be answering him in *Idler* No. 4 when he says that

compassion is by some reasoners, on whom the name of philosophers has been too easily conferred, resolved into an affection merely selfish, an involuntary perception of pain at the involuntary sight of a being like ourselves languishing in misery. But this sensation, if it ever be felt at all from the brute instinct of uninstructed nature, will only produce effects desultory and transient; it will never settle into a principle of action, or extend relief to calamities unseen, in generations not yet in being.[15]

Johnson has some qualities in common with Mandeville, and at times seems to be fighting the same battle, but one thing he does not share is Mandeville's irrationalism. Although he is willing enough to believe men are evil and to blame their evil actions on the passions, he refuses to attribute the bulk of their good deeds wholly to either instinct, appetite, or emotion.

2

Beneficence begins with the relationship between individuals, and Johnson speaks so frequently of this phase of righteousness that it is difficult to know what examples to choose. The most fervid sermons, for instance, are those dealing with personal charity. The peroration to the fourth Sermon, which was preached at Bath, is typical of Johnson's impassioned manner of treating the subject:

Remember thou! that now faintest under the weight of long-continued

---

[14] "An Essay on Charity and Charity Schools," in *The Fable of the Bees,* edited by F. B. Kaye (2 vols.; Oxford, 1924), I, 253 and 254.
[15] *Works,* IV, 160–161.

maladies, that to thee, more emphatically, the night cometh in which no man can work; and therefore, say not to him that asketh thee, "Go away now, and to-morrow I will give." To-morrow! To-morrow is to *all* uncertain, to *thee* almost hopeless; to-*day* if thou wilt hear the voice of God calling thee to repentance, and by repentance to charity, harden not thy heart; but what thou knowest that in thy last moment thou shalt wish done, make haste to do, lest thy last moment shall be upon thee.[16]

Johnson deals just as vigorously with those whose neglect of the obligations of beneficence stems mainly from indifference toward the world about them rather than from moral lethargy or avarice. Perhaps the best known example is Gelidus, who was so busy with his meteorological observations that he did not notice that a nearby town was afire and its inhabitants in need of assistance, and who was not concerned when he did find out. "Thus lives this great philosopher, insensible to every spectacle of distress, and unmoved by the loudest call of social nature, for want of considering that men are designed for the succour and comfort of each other." [17] Thus, Johnson has several reasons for scoffing at the escapist or recluse, but from a moral point of view, one predominates. As he says of religious hermits in *Adventurer* No. 126,

Piety practised in solitude, like that flower that blooms in the desert, may give its fragrance to the winds of Heaven, and delight those unbodied spirits that survey the works of God and the actions of men; but it bestows no assistance upon earthly beings, and however free of the taints of impurity, yet wants the sacred splendour of beneficence.[18]

Indeed, piety practised in solitude can never be more than half-effective because, "the power of godliness is contained in the love of God and of our neighbour; in that sum of religion, in which, as we are told by the Saviour of the world, the law and the prophets are comprised." [19]

Toward those who are positively evil in their relationships with

---

[16] *Works,* IX, 330. See also Sermons XI and XX.
[17] *Works,* II, 120 (*Rambler* No. 24).
[18] *Works,* IV, 127.
[19] *Works,* IX, 411 (Sermon XIII).

others, rather than indifferent, those who are completely given over to "that self-love, which dazzles all mankind," [20] Johnson is as bitter as any of his contemporaries, but he differs in two respects from some eighteenth-century proponents of the ethics of benevolence. First, he does not oversimplify the problem of the respective merits of self-love and social. One of the liabilities involved in passing over the prudential phase of Johnson's moralizing is that doing so tends to emphasize the importance of social love at the expense of the other form and makes the problem seem a matter of white and black; whereas, Johnson actually believes that a mean or balance between the two forces is desirable. To anyone who defined virtue wholly in terms of other-regarding emotions, Johnson would be certain to point out in his hardheaded way that he who does not take care of his own interests is not likely to have any opportunity of advancing those of others.

The other respect in which Johnson differs from many contemporaries in his attitude toward self-love is his conviction that in most men it is predominant and ineradicable; in this he agrees with Mandeville. Unlike many who made morality consist in benevolence, Johnson does not confuse what men ought to do, with what they actually do and are liable to continue doing. In *Rambler* No. 64 he states that

multitudes are unqualified for a constant and warm reciprocation of benevolence, as they are incapacitated for any other elevated excellence, by perpetual attention to their interest, and unresisting subjection to their passions.[21]

No matter how powerful the altruistic spirit is in some men, mankind is by nature subject to opposing forces:

we are formed for society, not for combination; we are equally unqualified to live in a close connexion with our fellow-beings, and in total separation from them; we are attracted towards each other by

[20] *Works,* VI, 407 (Life of Sydenham).
[21] *Works,* II, 305.

general sympathy, but kept back from contact by private interests.[22]

That Johnson acknowledges the persistence and dominance of self-love does not mean that he condones those who lack social affections, however; one need go no further than the *Ramblers* to find a whole gallery of malevolent folk who are exhibited in order that we may scorn them and their ways. They are easily as monstrous as any of those villains in the fiction of the day, whose blackness makes the Squire Allworthys seem all the more lustrous. Johnson often packs a number of the creatures into one brief narrative by the device of having some guileless hero or heroine encounter one after the other. Repressing credulity in the young may be the chief purpose of some of his epistolary narratives of this type, but others Johnson obviously wrote to condemn the heartless. In *Rambler* No. 12, for instance, Zosima, the daughter of a country gentleman reduced in circumstances, comes to London seeking work. Her misfortunes are first mocked by her cousin and then by Mrs. Bombasine, a great silk-mercer's lady. When Zosima applies to Mrs. Standish, this lady asks, "What brought you to town, a bastard?" and suggests she turn to the Foundling-house; Lady Lofty recommends the taverns. Finally, Mr. and Mrs. Courtly so much enjoy making sport of the girl and humiliating her that they fall into "the most violent agitations of delight." Eubulus encounters more individuals of this stripe in *Rambler* No. 26 and No. 27 as do Hymenaeus and Misella in other issues.[23]

Interest is the spur which drives some of these malefactors, like the haberdasher of whom Misocapelus says, "My master, who had no conception of any virtue, merit, or dignity, but that of being rich, had all the good qualities which naturally arise from a close and unwearied attention to the main chance."[24] More

---

[22] *Works*, IV, 18 (*Adventurer* No. 45).
[23] In No. 113 and No. 170–171. For a sampling of other heartless monsters see *Rambler* 46, 55, 74, 149, 197 and 198.
[24] *Works*, III, 51 (*Rambler* No. 116).

complex motives account for the venomous Squire Bluster of No. 142. But however they come to be that way, Johnson seems to feel that all those who are utterly consumed with self-love and who flout the rule of benevolence deserve no better than the poetic justice which fell upon Bluster,

a man in whose power fortune has liberally placed the means of happiness, but who has defeated all her gifts of their end by the depravity of his mind. He is wealthy without followers; he is magnificent without witnesses; he has birth without alliance, and influence without dignity. His neighbors scorn him as a brute; his dependants dread him as an oppressor; and he has only the gloomy comfort of reflecting, that if he is hated, he is likewise feared.[25]

[25] *Works,* III, 177.

$\{$ IV $\}$

Utility and Altruism

Johnson's strictures on the malevolence of some individuals toward others are the sort of reaction we might expect from any compassionate person. On the other hand, while this same compassion is evident in much of Johnson's social thinking, his attitudes on questions where society as a whole is involved usually derive just as much from a reasoned and more or less systematic group of principles. In the broader applications of beneficence it is more than ever obvious that the *results* of actions count the most with him. For example, in the sixth Sermon, as a prologue to his remarks on pride as a form of self-love, Johnson sets up two definitions. The first is narrow:

Pride, simply considered, is an immoderate degree, of self-esteem, or an over-value set upon a man by himself, and, like most other vices, is founded originally on an intellectual falsehood. But this definition sets this vice in the fairest light, and separates it from all its consequences, by considering man without relation to society, and independent of all outward circumstances. . . . In speculation, pride may be considered as ending where it began, and exerting no influence beyond the bosom in which it dwells; but in real life, and the course of affairs, pride will always be attended with kindred passions, and produce effects equally injurious to others, and destructive to itself.[1]

In other words, Squire Bluster's vicious temperament is certainly reprehensible, but from a practical point of view it is the effect of Bluster's malevolence on others which is crucial morally.

Now, in Johnson's case this sort of thinking applied to man in "relation to society" as a whole results in an attitude which is most precisely described as altruistic utilitarianism, repellent though the term may be. This attitude is altruistic because the most praiseworthy and efficient motive to the desired end is considered to be benevolence, which is, accordingly, the cause. It is utilitarian because the effect, the ultimate criterion, is the benefits which result for the members of society.

Although the principle can be neatly summed up in a phrase, the applications are subtle and complex, and the most formidable problem in discussing them is to maintain some degree of objectivity. To discuss Johnson's ideas in a historical vacuum, is to risk falling into a number of prevalent errors, blameless perhaps, but undesirable certainly. There is the risk of applying present-day political, social, and economic criteria to his notions unfairly, in a context where such criteria have no meaning. Or, what is worse, there is the danger of making Johnson's thought anew so that it will be more relevant to our own situation. And, finally, there is the common foible of regarding as distinctively Johnsonian, ideas which he actually shared with a number of his contemporaries. Since I have perforce renounced any attempt to describe Johnson's intellectual milieu, the most feasible way of maintaining some perspective is occasionally to compare his notions with those of a similar moralist who is more systematic

[1] *Works,* IX, 344.

and whose relation to the current of ideas is more easily recognizable.

At first glance, the ethical system of Richard Cumberland (1632–1718) may seem a rather odd choice for this purpose because his sole ethical work, *De legibus naturae,* was published in 1672, but for several reasons this treatise is especially suitable. For one thing Johnson owned *De legibus naturae,*[2] he read it,[3] and he recommended it.[4] Again, most eighteenth-century moralists who emphasize altruism base their systems on emotion or some other nonrational aspect of mind, and, whatever the other similarities, this antithetical element makes comparison with Johnson difficult. Cumberland is a rationalist in morals; moreover, his concept of reason is very close to that of Johnson, which I described in the first chapter. It is probable, too, that Johnson derived some of his notions from Cumberland, although, because these ideas were the common property of so many moralists, it would be difficult to prove his indebtedness. We shall see, however, that whether or not Cumberland was the immediate source of certain of Johnson's ethical notions, he was very likely their ultimate source. The comparison is also fitting because Johnson was clearly influenced by the classical seventeenth-century writers on natural law—the older generation who were more interested in the laws of nature than in the rights of man—and Cumberland is the most important English member of this group. Finally, even if we ignore Johnson's tendency to look to the past for his moral ideas, there is no real anachronism involved in comparing him with this particular seventeenth-century moralist, for *De legibus naturae* was one of those rare books which are written far ahead of their time. It did not become popular until the times

[2] See *A Catalogue of the valuable Library of Books of the late learned Samuel Johnson, Esq; LLD* (1892), p. 5, item 61, where it is listed under the name of one of its translators, John Towers.

[3] See *Idler* No. 36, for instance.

[4] *Works,* V, 244 (Preface to the *Preceptor*).

caught up with it, in the eighteenth century.[5] Cumberland is largely neglected now, but not because anything has come to light that detracts from those generous estimates of his importance to the history of thought, which were made from fifty to seventy-five years ago.[6] Frank Chapman Sharp, who established Cumberland's influence on Samuel Clarke, Shaftesbury, and ,others, calls him "one of the three or four most powerful influences in the history of British ethics."[7] Frank E. Spaulding's opinion is apparent from the title of his Leipzig dissertation *Richard Cumberland als Begründer der englischen Ethik* (1894). Perhaps the best discussion is by Ernest Albee who devotes fifty pages of *A History of English Utilitarianism* (1902) to Cumberland; and considers him the originator of the movement, as did the great Henry Sidgwick, who called him the "founder of English Utilitarianism."[8]

The influential parts of Cumberland's system are by-products of what was the most successful reply to Thomas Hobbes. One reason for its success was that, despite Cumberland's piety and his propensity for abstractions, his attack was neither religious like Archbishop Bramhall's nor metaphysical like that of the

---

[5] This is borne out by its publishing history. It was twenty years before an English translation, in the form of an authorized "abridgement" of 396 pages, was published. Two years later, in 1694, the Latin version reached what was apparently its third edition with a printing in Frankfort. The translation was re-edited in 1701. A new translation was made in 1727 by John Maxwell and another by John Towers in ·1750, which was the one Johnson owned. Meanwhile, the first French edition had appeared in Amsterdam in 1744, and there was demand sufficient for a reissue at Leyden in 1757. Thus, although only two editions of *De legibus naturae* were issued during the two decades after the book was first published, seven editions appeared, well-spaced, during the subsequent sixty-five years.

[6] Cumberland, great-grandfather of his dramatist namesake, was incidentally a good friend of Pepys, and Samuel's favorite candidate for the hand of sister Pall, despite his rustic appearance. And Pepys showed good judgment, for the erudite Cumberland turned out better than Mr. Jackson, spending the last twenty-seven years of a long and successful life, as bishop of Peterborough.

[7] "The Ethical System of Richard Cumberland and its place in the history of British Ethics," *Mind*, N.S., XXI (1912), 371.

[8] *The Methods of Ethics* (1890), p. 420.

Cambridge Platonists; instead, it was wholly ethical, aimed directly at Hobbes's fundamental assumptions. And underneath a lamentably nebulous organization was concealed the strength of simplicity, for Cumberland reduced the Laws of Nature to a single proposition:

The greatest Benevolence of every rational Agent towards all, forms the happiest State of every, and of all the Benevolent, as far as in their Power; and is necessarily requisite to the happiest State which they can attain, and therefore the common Good is the supreme Law.

Although this proposition is stated in terms of benevolent motives, Cumberland is strictly utilitarian, for it is the results of the action based on the motive which make us call it good: "Virtue is therefore Good . . . because it determines Human Actions to such effects, as are principal parts of the Public *Natural Good*." [9]

Cumberland, then, agrees with Hobbes that men need society but he disagrees as to its bases. Men are certainly egoistic; especially in a primitive state, but self-preservation is not an adequate *ideal* or *end* for a complex society. Only an altruistic devotion to the common good will serve this pupose; only to this will the common opinion of mankind assent. Furthermore, although self-love may be dominant in man, it does not sum up the whole of his nature, for in every man is the seed of sympathy for his fellows, a seed which when properly nurtured can make altruism dominant. These were replies to Hobbes which, during the eighteenth century, the growing host of optimists concerning human nature wanted to hear. And the practical utilitarian aspect of the greatest happiness principle, the fact that Cumberland laid the groundwork for reconciling self-love with social, must have attracted even more admirers to *De legibus naturae*.

As we turn first to consider briefly Johnson's theory of society as a purely political structure, it is in this utilitarian point of view that we will find the closest parallels between the two men. Al-

[9] *The Laws of Nature,* pp. 41, 197–198.

though Johnson frequently comments on the origin and purposes of government, there are no extensive discussions of the subject in his works. He says more in Sermon XXIV than anywhere else.

> Man is, for the most part, equally unhappy, when subjected, without redress, to the passions of another, or left, without control, to the dominion of his own. This every man, however unwilling he may be to own it of himself, will very readily acknowledge of his neighbour. No man knows anyone, except himself, whom he judges fit to be set free from the coercion of laws, and to be abandoned to his own choice. . . . Government is, therefore, necessary, in the opinion of everyone, to the safety of particular men, and the happiness of society.[10]

It is apparent that a state of nature is, more or less, a state of war and that the immediate purpose, at least, "of all civil regulations is to secure private happiness from private malignity; to keep individuals from the power of one another." [11]

On the surface, there would not seem to be much to choose between this theory of the origin and purpose of political institutions and that of Thomas Hobbes, but there are decisive, though subtle, differences. In the first place, some such common sense basis for the origin of society is espoused by many of the traditionalists who opposed Hobbes. For instance, Puffendorf, another exponent of natural law whom Johnson recommends,[12] believes that "the genuine and principal reason why the patriarchs, abandoning their natural liberty, took to founding states, was that they might fortify themselves against the evils which threaten man from man." [13] Secondly, a crucial difference is that Johnson, like Cumberland, stresses the hope of good as a motive in the formation of states. As he says in *Idler* No. 36, "the ultimate pur-

---

[10] *Works*, IX, 507.

[11] *Works*, IV, 214.

[12] In the preface to the *Preceptor*. He was well enough acquainted with Puffendorf to cite him in *Life*, II, 157.

[13] *De officio hominis et civis juxta legem naturalem libri duo*, translated by Frank G. Moore (New York, 1927), II, 104. First published in 1673. Puffendorf was influenced by Hobbes, but remained opposed to him on most of the fundamental issues with which we will be concerned.

pose of government is temporal, and that of religion is eternal happiness." Hobbes, on the other hand, always insists on the fear of evil: *"societatis civilis initium esse a mutuo metu."* [14]

Cumberland is not splitting hairs when he berates Hobbes for depending on fear rather than hope, because this distinction which seems to arise from a slight semantic shift is actually the surface indication of a broad and fundamental division between the two schools. No matter how deeply pessimistic Johnson, and those proponents of natural law to whom I am comparing him, may seem concerning man's selfishness—and Puffendorf and Johnson at times come very close to Hobbes in this respect—they also feel that man has some natural affinity for his fellows, an affinity which Hobbes believes to be nonexistent. I have already cited the passage from *Adventurer* No. 45, beginning, "we are formed for society . . . ," where Johnson tries to sum up the centrifugal and centripetal forces involved. *Rambler* No. 99 is wholly devoted to the forces which draw men together:

As the perpetuity and distinction of the lower tribes of creation require that they should be determined to proper mates by some uniform motive of choice, or some cogent principle of instinct, it is necessary, likewise, that man, whose wider capacity demands more gratifications . . . should be led to suitable companions by particular influence; and among many beings of the same nature with himself, he may select some for intimacy and tenderness, and improve the condition of his existence, by superadding friendship to humanity, and the love of individuals to that of the species.[15]

Hugo Grotius, master of both Puffendorf and Cumberland, draws a very similar analogy.[16] Speaking generally of all the attractive forces, he says that

[14] The rubric of part ii, chap. I of *De cive.*

[15] *Works,* II, 468–469.

[16] Some readers will remember that Grotius was peculiarly distinguished among those whom Johnson admired. As Mrs. Thrale tells it, "We were saying that . . . no Man would change himself—that is his own Character all together, person Mind—Chance for Eternity tout ensemble with any other Man or Woman living or dead. Johnson said he would change with nobody but Hugo Grotius" (*Thraliana,* I, 377). For his reasons and for his knowledge of the works of Grotius see the index to the *Life.*

among the traits characteristic of man is an impelling desire for society, that is, for the social life—not of any and every sort, but peaceful, and organized according to the measure of his intelligence, with those who are of his own kind; this social trend the Stoics called "sociableness." Stated as a universal truth, therefore, the assertion that every animal is impelled by nature to seek only its own good cannot be conceded. Some of the other animals, in fact, do in a way restrain the appetency for that which is good for themselves alone, to the advantage, now of their offspring, now of other animals of the same species.[17]

Parallels to this testament of faith in man's social instincts written by Grotius in 1625 are to be found in the works of many of those who later opposed natural law to Hobbism. This same notion, which Shaftesbury used to rationalize his sentimental benevolism, can be traced in the thought of more sober humanitarians such as Johnson, and it sets all the altruistic moralists apart from Hobbes and his followers, such as Mandeville.

Among the other ways in which Johnson's concept of the origin and purpose of government differs from that of Hobbes and resembles that of Cumberland is one which is especially decisive, Johnson's feeling that even a state of nature is subject to a transcendent law. This is very well illustrated by his comments in Aberdeen on the statute of limitations as applied to murder:

If the son of the murdered man should kill the murderer who got off merely by prescription, I would help him to make his escape; though, were I upon his jury, I would not acquit him. I would not advise him to commit such an act. On the contrary, I would bid him submit to the determination of society, because a man is bound to submit to the inconveniences of it, as he enjoys the good: but the young man, though politically wrong, would not be morally wrong. He would have to say, "Here I am amongst barbarians, who not only refuse to do justice, but encourage the greatest of all crimes. I am therefore in a state of nature; for, so far as there is no law, it is a state of nature: and consequently, upon the eternal and immutable law of justice,

[17] *De jure belli ac pacis libri tres,* translated by Francis W. Kelsey (Oxford, 1925), II, 11. Grotius is perhaps more optimistic concerning the effectiveness of "sociableness" than Johnson.

which requires that he who sheds man's blood should have his blood shed, I will stab the murderer of my father.[18]

Even with all the careful qualifications this is rather an extreme line for Johnson to take, but there is no doubt that he is sincerely describing his feelings with regard to a state of nature. In it there is the paradox of law and no law, no positive, political law yet another law described as "eternal and immutable," a favorite phrase among the anti-Hobbists.[19]

The obligation to submit to the "determination of society" is based ultimately on the utility which political society was created to serve, which makes it none the less binding. Johnson merely points out that conflict is possible between positive law and the transcendent law, although it is not correct for the individual citizen to determine things for himself and act as if he were bound only by the transcendent law.

No conflict is possible in the system of Hobbes, for although he admits the existence of the laws of nature, he so qualifies them that they become meaningless and without force. For instance, they are not binding in a state of nature because it is a state of war, and in a civilized state they are, in effect, subordinate to civil laws:

By the virtue of the natural law which forbids breach of covenant, the law of nature commands us to keep all the civil laws. For where we are tied to obedience before we know what will be commanded us, there we are universally tied to obey in all things. Whence it follows, that no civil law whatsoever, which tends not to a reproach of the Deity, (in respect of whom cities themselves have no right of their own, and cannot be said to make laws), can possibly be against the law of nature. For though the law of nature forbid theft, adultery, &c; yet if the civil law command us to invade anything, that invasion is not theft, adultery, &c.[20]

[18] *Life,* V, 87–88.
[19] Compare the title of one of Ralph Cudworth's works, *A Treatise concerning Eternal and Immutable Morality.*
[20] *The English Works of Thomas Hobbes,* edited by Sir William Molesworth (1839–1845), II, 190–191. (*De cive* XIV, x).

Cumberland replies that civil power is prohibited from *"over-turning those other Laws of Nature,* for preserving which it is it-self founded, and to which the whole Security and Happiness of Rulers is owing." [21] It is because of this lack of transcendent law that Johnson considers Hobbism as synonymous with law-lessness. Thus Hume "has no principle. If he is any thing, he is a Hobbist." [22]

There is an interesting corollary to this rejection of Hobbesian lawless state of nature, a corollary which is relevant to the general point I am trying to make, that Johnson's political theory is essen-tially utilitarian. Since civil law is the only law in the system of Hobbes, the state is absolute, and, once we accept the law of na-ture regarding covenants, it tends to become an end in itself. This is not possible when a transcendent law is recognized as operative at all times, for this law acts as a check, and, as Cumber-land puts it, "the Civil Power is naturally and necessarily *limited* by the same End for which it is established," the end which Johnson defines as "the safety of particular men and the happi-ness of society."

Donald J. Greene would thus seem to deny this ultimate moral purpose to Johnson's political system, when, in his excellent *The Politics of Samuel Johnson,* he states that Johnson conceives of "the state as a purely secular and rational institution" which "is at least as atheistic as Hobbes'." Indeed, he thinks that in "dis-carding or ignoring the notion of contract" Johnson outdoes Hobbes to make sheer power the basis of the state. "Johnson is,

---

[21] *The Laws of Nature,* p. 351.

[22] *Life,* V, 272. Howard Warrender in the chapter on "The Laws of Nature and the Civil Law" in his valuable *The Political Philosophy of Thomas Hobbes* (Oxford, 1957) shows that for Hobbes the relation between the two forms of law is in theory much more subtle and complex than I can indicate here. I suspect, however, that the practical effects of such dicta of Hobbes as I have cited are about as I have described them, and, what is more important here, mine is the way in which Hobbes's contemporary opponents understood him. John Bowle, in the last chapter of his study of seventeenth-century constitutionalism, *Hobbes and his Critics* (New York, 1952), gives a useful summary of the issues as the opponents of Hobbes's political theories saw them.

in fact, in advance of most of his contemporaries in seeing and clearly stating the fact of the omnicompetence of the modern state." [23]

While I agree that Johnson's concept of the state is thoroughly utilitarian, I think that to assume therefore that Johnson is a Hobbist is merely to confuse matters by equating the political terms and presuppositions of the eighteenth century with those of the seventeenth. For instance, most of this part of Greene's discussion is drawn from *Taxation no Tyranny* and similar pamphlets of the 1770's, and it is true that some of the arguments regarding sovereignty and subordination which Johnson resorts to in these works are to be found in Hobbes, but so are they to be found in the writings of many of Hobbes's opponents who were supporters of natural law. In the form which Johnson propounds them, these ideas are neither novel nor modern—they are, in fact, commonplaces of seventeenth-century political theory which Johnson is using to refute eighteenth-century doctrinaire theorists.

Perhaps Greene does not mean to imply that Johnson in repudiating the concept of natural rights and like abstractions of his own day is also rejecting completely the notion of natural law which had been popular in the previous century. We can be certain, however, that Johnson the moralist was sensitive enough to the issues involved that it would be impossible for him to be an unconscious Hobbist, and to be a conscious Hobbist is consciously to reject something absolutely fundamental to the thought of Hooker, Grotius, and Cumberland.

It seems logical enough to lump together old and new as "the fine metaphysical theories of the seventeenth and eighteenth centuries," to equate, as Greene does, the older natural law with "Burkean ideas of prescription and the organic nature of the state" and with theories of divine right and natural right, as a system which also seeks to impose upon society *ab extra* a set of

[23] (New Haven, 1960), pp. 246, 215.

a priori abstract principles,[24] and to contrast it to the more empirical and utilitarian systems of Johnson and of Hobbes. Men more rapidly change their ideas than the terms which they use to describe them, and this lag can create an appearance of ideological stability or continuity where sometimes not even the latter exists. In reality, those particular authorities on natural law to whom Johnson was indebted—it was not for nothing that he would rather be Hugo Grotius than anyone else—were not airy metaphysicians, whatever their extravagances; they were economical of postulates and their writings were hardheadedly practical enough to become one of the prime sources of Johnson's own utilitarian notions.[25] Furthermore, what Johnson borrowed from them, directly or indirectly, was not the elaborate superstructure characteristic of some of their systems—of those, say, of Puffendorf and Grotius—but rather a few fundamental principles, derivable in turn from two or three presuppositions. When Greene contends that "where Johnson chiefly follows Hooker is in basing his scheme of society on the two postulates, that man is a social animal, and that obedience to authority is the essence of society," and proves this contention from the legal lectures which Johnson wrote for Robert Chambers, he grants Johnson all that is necessary to a belief in natural law, and that which of necessity incisively distinguishes him from a Hobbist.[26] Fundamentally, the law of nature is the law of human nature, and those of its advocates whom Johnson most admired based their theories on what they regarded as a simple psychological fact, this sociability. As Grotius puts it, *"naturalis juris mater est ipsa humana natura."* [27]

Of course, much depends upon how natural law is defined. If, for instance, it is thought of as some complex body of abstract

[24] Pages 256–257 and 195.

[25] Greene traces the greatest happiness principle as far back as Francis Hutcheson but does not note that Hutcheson borrowed it ultimately from Cumberland.

[26] *Politics,* pp. 194–195.

[27] *De jure belli et pacis libri tres* (Oxford, 1925), fol. 5, verso.

principles which govern the behavior of men in society, Johnson could hardly have any faith in it and at the same time be so pragmatic and utilitarian in his approach to political and social problems. On the other hand, if *nature* means *human nature,* as it did to the thinkers who most profoundly influenced Johnson, and natural law, accordingly, signifies certain very simple principles of behavior towards others, present, but not dominant, in the human psyche, tendencies which mankind will more or less uniformly concede to be correct and beneficial, because, as Johnson always insists, the essential nature of mankind is everywhere the same; then, there need be no conflict. Although this concept involves epistemological difficulties—no more perplexing, certainly, than those which confront moralists of our day—it seems unlikely that its proponents would regard it as incompatible with a utilitarian approach to the problems of society. One need only reflect that the most eminent English writer on natural law has been with some justice styled the father of utilitarianism.

The two postulates of authority and the social nature of man which Greene cites from Hooker also define the poles between which Johnson's and, for that matter, Cumberland's discussions of political society tend to fluctuate. And the fact of this fluctuation accounts, I think, for the seeming disagreement between Greene and myself, a disagreement which, when it is viewed in this light, is seen to be more apparent than real and largely the product of a difference in methodologies. The political pamphlets of the 1770's which suggest to Greene that Johnson outdoes Hobbes are partisan documents directed against a faction which constantly appealed to theory and to abstract principles.[28] In such a situation Johnson logically resorts to a common sense argument based upon the hard facts of power. He stresses author-

---

[28] According to Edward L. McAdam's *Doctor Johnson and the English Law* (Syracuse, N.Y., 1951), pp. 74–83, natural law seems to form an integral part of the system of law outlined in the Vinerian Lectures on which Johnson collaborated with Robert Chambers. For a list of books on natural law which were owned by Johnson, see p. 60 of Professor McAdam's book.

ity and positive law heavily, and the social nature of man and transcendent moral law, not at all. It follows that any political theory derived from these pamphlets must seem completely detached from a moral basis. But Johnson does not even temporarily abandon morality and thus become a part-time Hobbist or Machiavel. He is merely exercising the moralist's license to stress the phase of truth which is relevant, and, in any case, as Greene would certainly admit, the notion that one could have a political theory completely divorced from other considerations would not even occur to Johnson, although today we have come to take such compartmentalization more or less for granted. As we shall see, if the writings of the 1770's are seen in the larger context of what Johnson had to say about men in society, it is obvious that the social nature of man is as basic to Johnson's thinking as is the principle of authority.

2

When we leave this question of the ultimate bases and origins of political society and turn to the more important matter of Johnson's stand on the problems of the state once it is set up, Greene and I are in solid agreement as to the utilitarian nature of Johnson's arguments—and it is reassuring that different methods applied to what are for the most part different phases of the Johnsonian canon produce such unanimity.

Johnson's familiar pronouncements upon the subject of liberty and authority form a logical point of departure for considering this utilitarian habit of thought. Bertrand H. Bronson in his illuminating study, "Johnson Agonistes," remarks that what Johnson wants is "authority, and more authority . . . in Religion, in Morals, in Politics, in Literature." [29] And he cites the well-known passage from *Taxation no Tyranny:*

In sovereignty there are no gradations. There may be limited royalty, there may be limited consulship; but there can be no limited govern-

[29] *Johnson Agonistes and Other Essays* (Cambridge, 1946), p. 7. See also Joseph Wood Krutch's *Samuel Johnson* (New York, 1944), pp. 24–26.

ment. There must, in every society, be some power or other, from which there is no appeal, which admits no restrictions, which pervades the whole mass of the community, regulates and adjusts all subordination, enacts laws or repeals them, erects or annuls judicatures, extends or contracts privileges, exempt itself from question or control, and bound only by physical necessity.[30]

Bronson gives what is a plausible enough explanation of why Johnson insists that this ultimate power is necessary, when he ascribes the insistence to Johnson's "conservatism of intellectual attitude," and it may be unwise to probe further. Yet, although we have already seen abundant evidence that this conservative attitude dominates his moral notions, calling such beliefs conservative does not completely explain them, because they are in reality too complex to be comprehended in a single term and because behind the simple fact of their conservatism may lie another stratum of motives.

It is clear, for example, that behind Johnson's political conservatism, as is so often the case, there lies a deep-rooted fear of instability. The passage just quoted from *Taxation no Tyranny* comes from a section where Johnson is arguing hypothetically that the charters of the various colonies can be repealed by the Crown. At the end of the argument he pictures what would happen if this came about:

by such repeal the whole fabrick of subordination is immediately destroyed, and the constitution sunk at once into a chaos; the society is dissolved into a tumult of individuals, without authority to command, or obligation to obey, without any punishment of wrongs, but by personal resentment, or any protection of right, but by the hand of the possessor.[31]

This fear that the framework of society is brittle and easily destroyed, that men are always in danger of slipping back into a chaotic state of nature, Johnson sometimes justifies by pointing to the conflict between Parliament and Charles I:

This strife, as we all know, ended in confusion. Our laws were over-

[30] *Works*, VI, 234.
[31] *Works*, VI, 236

ruled, our rights were abolished. The soldier seized upon property, the fanatick rushed into the church. The usurpers gave way to other usurpers; the schismaticks were thrust out by other schismaticks; the people felt nothing from their masters but alternatives of oppression, and heard nothing from their teachers but varieties of errour.[32]

The ultimately absolute authority of the state derives from the practical necessity of preventing such disasters as these, not from any abstract principle. Accordingly, Johnson's state, unlike that of Hobbes, which itself defines the right, can and, as most readers of Johnson know, does do wrong. This he admits even in *Taxation no Tyranny*. The evil it may commit can be of two types, and some caution is necessary because Johnson does not always distinguish them. The act of the man who killed his father's murderer, after he had been released by prescription was described as "politically wrong" though "not morally wrong." This distinction applies especially to acts of the state and its agents. On one occasion when Boswell "introduced the subject of toleration," Johnson made the following remarks:

Every society has a right to preserve publick peace and order, and therefore has a good right to prohibit the propagation of opinions which have a dangerous tendency. To say the *magistrate* has this right, is using an inadequate word: it is the *society* for which the magistrate is agent. He may be morally or theologically wrong in restraining the propagation of opinions which he thinks dangerous, but he is politically right.[33]

Since political institutions have a moral purpose, Johnson often speaks simply of what is expedient for their preservation as right and what is destructive as wrong. However, when civil law comes into conflict with the transcendent law, Johnson is usually careful to distinguish between the former as concerned with political value and the latter with moral ends.

We have already seen an instance where society could be politically right though morally wrong. If Johnson were on the

[32] *Works*, IX, 505 (Sermon XXIII).
[33] *Life*, II, 249.

jury deciding the case of the boy who revenged his father he would not acquit him, for the young man should have submitted to the determination of society. The punishment of the innocent can be politically right, no matter how wrong it may be morally, for

> the objection, in which is urged the injustice of making the innocent suffer with the guilty, is an objection not only against society, but against the possibility of society. All societies, great and small, subsist upon this condition; that as the individuals derive advantages from union, they may likewise suffer inconveniences.[34]

Cumberland also argues "that this conduces more to the common Happiness, That a *few* should suffer that Evil, which may follow from an *unjust Sentence* . . . than that Strifes should never be ended, but by *Wars*." [35] In others words, choose what you will have, occasional injustice to a few or perpetual injustice for most, the state of nature.

In a quotation from *Taxation no Tyranny* with which we began this discussion of the dilemma of liberty and authority, Johnson stated that the supreme power in a state, whatever it may be, can do no political wrong and Cumberland concurs.[36] But what happens if a subordinate, an agent of society commits an act which is both morally and politically wrong against another member of society? Johnson would certainly grant redress to the sufferer and punish the offender, but if neither of these two things could be done it would be no impeachment of society. When Imlac says of his father, who sounds suspiciously Whiggish, that "he was honest, frugal and diligent, but of mean sentiments, and narrow comprehension: he desired only to be rich, and to conceal his riches, lest he should be spoiled by the governours of the province," the prince protests and receives a typically Johnsonian reply. Rasselas says,

[34] *Life*, II, 373–374.
[35] *The Laws of Nature*, p. 78.
[36] *The Laws of Nature*, p. 351.

My blood boils when I am told that a merchant durst not enjoy his honest gains for fear of losing them by the rapacity of power. Name the governour who robbed the people, that I may declare his crimes to the emperour.

Sir, said Imlac, your ardour is the natural effect of virtue animated by youth: the time will come when you will acquit your father [the emperour], and perhaps hear with less impatience of the governour. Oppression is, in the Abyssinian dominions, neither frequent nor tolerated; but no form of government has yet been discovered, by which cruelty can be wholly prevented. Subordination supposes power on one part and subjection on the other; and if power be in the hands of men, it will sometimes be abused. The vigilance of the supreme magistrate may do much, but much will still remain undone.[37]

Cumberland also argues

that they who are subject to the *same Human Government,* cannot be perfectly *Secure,* either that their *Fellow-Subjects* will observe the Laws of the State by abstaining from Rebellion, and all Invasion of another's property, or that their chief Governor will be both *able* to punish the Transgressors of his Laws, . . . and *willing* to take the greatest care he can of the Publick Good.

And his reasons are the same as Johnson's: "Whoever requires absolute or *perfect Security,* concerning *future Human Actions,* whether in a State of Nature, or under Civil Government, requires an *Impossibility;* for the Actions of Men are in their own Nature *Contingent.*" [38]

One of Imlac's qualifications must be taken note of, however, if we are to understand how Johnson feels about abuse of authority. Imlac remarks that "oppression is, in the Abyssinian dominions, neither frequent nor tolerated." In *Rasselas,* as elsewhere when he speaks on the dilemma of liberty and authority, Johnson is speaking in an English context. Even when he uses theoretical terms his opinions are influenced by the immediate practical situation. The abuses are not gross, but what he regards as small and infrequent, because he is convinced that "an Englishman in the common course of life and action feels no restraint."

[37] *Rasselas,* pp. 37–38.
[38] *The Laws of Nature,* p. 283.

In 1760 Johnson began his review of Tytler's *Enquiry* with the following statement:

We live in an age, in which there is much talk of independence, or private judgment, of liberty of thought, and liberty of press. Our clamourous praises of liberty sufficiently prove that we enjoy it; and if, by liberty, nothing else be meant, than security from the persecutions of power, it is so fully possessed by us, that little more is to be desired, except that one should talk of it less, and use it better.[39]

What if the abuses of authority are not minor, as they are in England, but extensive and involve not agents but the supreme authority of the state itself? Johnson replied to Goldsmith in 1763, that *"if the abuse be enormous, Nature will rise up, and claiming her original rights, overturn a corrupt political system."* And several years later he gave the same answer to Sir Adam Ferguson:

I consider that in no government power can be abused long. Mankind will not bear it. If a sovereign oppresses his people to a great degree, they will rise and cut off his head. There is a remedy in human nature against tyranny, that will keep us safe under every form of government.[40]

It was this "necessity of self-preservation" which "impelled the subjects of James to drive him from the throne." [41] Hawkins remarks with astuteness on Johnson's readiness to admit that the Revolution was necessary, although he disapproved of some of its results:

That he was a tory, he not only never hesitated to confess, but, by his frequent invectives against the Whigs, was forward to proclaim: yet, was he not so besotted in his notions, as to abett what is called the patriarchal scheme, as delineated by Sir Robert Filmer and other writers on government; nor, with others of a more sober cast, to acquiesce in the opinion that, because submission to governors is, in general terms, inculcated in the Holy Scriptures, the resistance of tyranny and oppression is, in all cases, unlawful: he seemed rather to adopt the sentiments of Hooker on the subject, as explained by

[39] *Works,* VI, 80.

[40] *Life,* I, 424; II, 170.

[41] *Works,* VI, 135 (The Political State of Great Britain). See also *Life,* III, 3, and IV, 170.

Hoadly, and, by consequence, to look on submission to lawful authority as a moral obligation.[42]

Hooker maintains that the authority of the governors originally arose from a compact assented to by the governed in order that they might procure "peace, tranquillity, and happy estate." [43]

Since the moral obligation to obey authority depends ultimately on the purposes for which government was instituted in the first place, it is difficult to see why Johnson's conviction that in some few extreme cases revolution may be justified, is "radically self-contradictory" or "goes far to undermine his whole doctrine," as Professor Bronson suggests. Results, not abstract principles or political articles of faith, are what he constantly appeals to. And when he argues that there must be somewhere in the state a supreme power—he never argues for the infallibility of subordinates—Johnson does so not because of a loyalty rational, emotional, or religious to some doctrine of authority, but because he fears the results if something less than complete supremacy allows the individual to set himself up as fittest arbiter of the collective good, which he is likely to interpret as synonymous with his private good. The supreme authority can be morally wrong, but the state so constituted that he can be politically wrong, even slightly, is like a dike which leaks slightly. However, if the purposes for which this authority was granted are decisively thwarted, the same human nature which made the authority necessary, will destroy it.

Happily, there is no need to defend Johnson's political theory, for, regardless of the shrewd insights into human affairs involved, it is intended for his day, not ours. In general, Johnson's English-speaking descendants do not share his fear that political society is always in danger of slipping back into a state of nature, at least from internal causes. And in a way this confidence is justified by his own notion that tyrannies are like inverted cones, easily top-

[42] *Life of Samuel Johnson* (1787), p. 504.
[43] *Of the Laws of Ecclesiastical Polity,* I, x, 4.

pled; whereas, the more broadly based, the more pyramidal, a society is, the more stable it is likely to be. On the other hand, there is one formidable barrier to ever understanding Johnson's political notions, our doctrinaire tendencies. Our political institutions often seem quite empirical and haphazard on the surface, yet when we are required to justify them we commonly resort to ultimate principles, natural rights and the like. Johnson has all the appearance of advocating an absolutism equally doctrinaire, but when he is forced to justify it he does so on the basis of utility. Macaulay confused means and ends when he became incensed because, despite his obvious partisanship, Johnson declares that he "would not give half a guinea to live under one form of government than another." In this instance, Johnson is merely asserting the primacy of the end, that the test of any government is the amount of personal liberty and security it achieves for the individual. He felt very strongly that these objectives were best attained if the government erred toward authority rather than liberty, since err it must, but he never lost sight of the end.

Johnson's statement of indifference regarding the form of government also illustrates another conviction which does not fit into the picture often drawn of him as being thoroughly doctrinaire in his political notions. Johnson feels that all goverenments are bad. This is one point on which he agrees with Soame Jenyns. Commenting on Jenyns's assertion that "from government, evils cannot be eradicated, and their excess only can be prevented," Johnson says "that this has been always allowed; the question, upon which all dissension arises, is when that excess begins, at what point men shall cease to bear, and attempt to remedy." And he approvingly quotes Jenyns's explanation of these evils, because the precept "cannot be too frequently impressed":

Every wise man ought to redress them to the utmost of his power; which can be effected by one method only, that is, by a reformation of manners; for, as all political evils derive their original from moral, these can never be removed, until those are first amended.

No doctrine or system can guarantee good government as long as human nature is what it is, and is likely to remain; hence, "the perpetual subject of political disquisition is not absolute, but comparative good." [44]

Johnson's attitude on both of the aspects of political theory which we have been considering, the origin of government and the dilemma of liberty and authority, is ultimately utilitarian. Government is necessary "to the safety of particular men and the happiness of society." "Every man who claims the protection of Society must purchase it by resigning some part of his natural right." Since the alternative is a state of war, it is better that governments lean toward severity rather than laxity, and, if political society is subject to abuses, "a man is bound to submit to the inconveniences of it as he enjoys the good." Societies are "never to be tried by a regular theory," for the good enjoyed by the members of society is the only real criterion.

3

Since most of this brief discussion of two phases of Johnson's political notions has been based on statements made during his later life, we have had no glimpse of that fiery young radical whom Bronson capably portrays in his "Johnson Agonistes." This phase of his career has been largely ignored because, for practical purposes it was already over when he commenced his work as a moralist. It is true that in an essay written in the *British Magazine* in 1760 he attributes the bravery of the English common soldier to "neglect of subordination," yet against this date as the *terminus ad quem* for Johnson's radicalism there is considerable evidence in the *Literary Magazine* for 1756, where he praises absolutism in terms which seem natural to the more familiar Johnson, but to the author of *Marmor Norfolciense,* impossible.[45]

[44] *Works,* VI, 74, 163 (*The False Alarm*).
[45] See for example the remarks on Colbert in the "Political State of Great

Bronson points out that after the fall of Walpole Johnson gradually became convinced that felicity depends not on kings or laws but on the moral behavior of the individual. The change was virtually complete by 1749, which James L. Clifford makes clear in comparing Johnson's two major poems:

London is a young man's poem. It breathes the ardor, the vehemence, the keen sense of right and wrong of youth. It is the work of a man newly come to the city, shocked by much of what he sees and still clinging to his early ideals, still hoping that a change of leadership may bring improvement. It has the impetuous zest of someone ready to throw himself into the political arena. A decade later, when next he imitated Juvenal, in *The Vanity of Human Wishes,* much of this youthful impetuosity would be gone. Ten years of poverty and struggle in London would complete his education.[46]

In this mature Johnson, Bronson suggests, the reverence for authority also became increasingly stronger and by 1760, dominant, as he reacted more and more vigorously against the growing influence of Rousseau and other innovators. Thus the older Johnson was just as much in revolt as the younger and, in one sense, it was the times which changed, not he. What sort of conservative does this thesis make Johnson? Is he to be identified with that image of conservatism which has been created to serve the changing temper of our own times—the enlightened, Burkean figure who conceives of society as a plastic, growing organism the proper development of which can be thwarted just as easily by the doctrinaires who wish to make the state supreme, as by those who champion individual rights at the expense of every other consideration? Up to a certain point—but not very far— it is possible to trace the parallel between the notions of Johnson and Burke, and, by doing so, make the older Johnson's ideas more palatable to the tastes of the present moment, but Bronson seems

---

Britain" (*Works*, VI, 133–134) and on the efficiency of French colonial policy in "Observations on the State of Affairs in 1756" (*Works*, VI, 121–122).

[46] *Young Sam Johnson*, p. 194. For a very perceptive discussion of this shift, see chap. V of Greene's *The Politics of Samuel Johnson*.

to have no intention of doing so. Actually, underlying his portrait of a Johnson who wrestled late, as well as early against popular political ideals, can be discerned that familiar stereotype created by contemporary political opponents, furthered by nineteenth-century Whigs, and perpetuated in our day by many critics less astute and perceptive than Professor Bronson—the image of a conservative who is wholly dogmatic rather than flexible, whose ideas derive more from blind conviction than calm deliberation, who thinks of society as a static hierarchy not an organism, and who, far from admitting the inevitability, much less the desirability, of change, obstinately clings to the past.

Johnson is all of these things at one time and another, and no such image can be expected to be congruent always with the individual it describes, but this generalization does not fulfill our minimal expectations. There are too many important occasions when it is absolutely impossible to make the image fit the man. We have already seen two such instances: Johnson's belief that if the supreme power commits enormous abuses, it should be overthrown, and his readiness to admit that all governments are bad. This notion of Johnson as devotee of authority for authority's sake becomes even more difficult to sustain if one examines closely his attitudes on those problems of society which are properly sociological and economic, rather than political. Bronson states that the mature Johnson was willing to help right a social wrong providing that "the principle of subordination" was not violated in the process. This he illustrates by pointing to Johnson's attacks on capital punishment and the debtor's laws. The best known of Johnson's protests, against slavery, he deals with more briefly, citing only an argument which he regards as curious coming from the pen of Johnson. Indeed, all of Johnson's arguments against slave-holding and the slave trade are curious if he is the sort of conservative which Bronson describes, because few men are more subversive of the principle of subordination than the abolitionist.

This reactionary stereotype has seemed all the more plausible because of Johnson's shift from political idealism to the moral approach as he grew older. To anyone accustomed to thinking of reform wholly in terms of political and social action, the moralist, who seeks to reform up from the individual, rather than from the top down, seems to propose no action at all, one way or the other, and therefore is certain to appear strongly conservative or reactionary. Often both Johnson's friends and his foes have sought to explain the fact that he continued to attack institutions long after he had shifted the blame from institutions to men, by ascribing these attacks to humanitarian impulses which occasionally ran counter to his reverence for authority. This seems to be Bronson's point of view, and it is a useful one, but it obscures the essential truth that the altruistic impulse is not something occasional; it is organic to Johnson's whole concept of society.

Actually there is no longer any need to reconcile the politics of a doggedly reactionary Johnson with his humanitarian sentiments, for Donald J. Greene in his *The Politics of Samuel Johnson* has forever laid to rest the traditional reactionary stereotype. In this admirably thorough study Greene follows the whole history of Johnson's political thinking, and there emerges a very convincing Johnson still conservative, but skeptical, pragmatic, and flexible in his conservatism, the antithesis of that remarkably persistent figure of a bigot portrayed by Macaulay.

Greene's achievement may make more acceptable my next contention: that we do not sufficiently reflect on the timing of Johnson's humanitarian protests, and that when we do we must completely reassess their significance with respect to his view of society. We may expect a diehard conservative to approve the results of previous changes in the structure of society; occasionally, we may find him jumping aboard the bandwagon when a change is already under way; but he ceases to be the sort of conservative Johnson is so often made out to be if he is ahead of the general public in his attitude toward changes in social institutions sanctified by law and hallowed by precedent, if he advocates, instead of accepting change. Especially is this true, if, as in Johnson's case, the changes do not in any sense represent a return to previous traditions or customs. One has to go back all the way to the Middle Ages to find even a feeble precedent for the charitable ferment which spread through England in the eighteenth century.

Let us consider a specific case. In March 1751, Johnson gave support to a project for the public reclamation of prostitutes, by publishing in *Rambler* No. 107 a moving letter on the subject, by his friend Joseph Simpson. Lock Hospital founded in 1746 could treat their diseases and attempt a religious conversion, but could not teach them some trade in order to keep them from falling back into their previous way of life. It was not until several years after the publication of this *Rambler,* the earliest printed plea Betsy Rodgers notes in her discussion of the topic,[47] that Robert Dingley and Jonas Hanway, a zealous reformer and certainly a man ahead of his time, began the public agitation which led to the founding of Magdalen Hospital to serve this purpose.

There had been considerable agitation for reform of the brutally stringent laws concerning debtors before Johnson wrote on the subject in 1753, but again Johnson was protesting long before any action was taken. It was 1759 before a permanent measure was passed for relief, a law palliative, at best, and not until 1772 was a charitable organization to succour debtors established.[48]

Johnson's first effort in this cause was *Adventurer* No. 62, a typical narrative epistle dated from the Fleet, in which he shows how grievously those "whose virtue has made them unhappy or whose misfortunes are at least without a crime" suffer under existing debtor's laws. After several examples he concludes, "yet

---

[47] *Cloak of Charity* (1949), p. 49. See also John H. Hutchins, *Jonas Hanway* (S.P.C.K., 1940), p. 112.

[48] Individuals, of course, had for a long time answered pleas in behalf of specific debtors and their families. See W. S. Lewis and Ralph M. Williams, *Private Charity in England, 1747–1757* (New Haven, 1938), pp. 58–67.

must these, with multitudes equally blameless, languish in confinement, till malevolence shall relent, or the law be changed." [49]
In *Idler* No. 22 Johnson maintains that "since poverty is punished amongst us as a crime, it ought at least to be treated with the same lenity as other crimes," and he concludes with a utilitarian argument:

It is vain to continue an institution, which experience shows to be ineffectual. We have now imprisoned one generation of debtors after another, but we do not find that their numbers lessen. We have now learned that rashness and imprudence will not be deterred from taking credit; let us try whether fraud and avarice may be more easily restrained from giving it.

In *Idler* No. 38 he appeals to altruism:

Surely, he whose debtor has perished in prison, although he may acquit himself of deliberate murder, must at least have his mind clouded with discontent, when he considers how much another has suffered from him; when he thinks on the wife bewailing her husband, or the children begging the bread which their father would have earned. If there are any made so obdurate by avarice or cruelty, as to revolve these consequences without dread or pity, I must leave them to be awakened by some other power, for I write only to human beings.[50]

Johnson seems to realize that he cannot expect to see a genuine reform of the law during his lifetime, so he recommends that if this is not now possible, public opinion should be remolded in order that he who imprisons anyone for debt "shall be hunted through the world as an enemy to man, and find in riches no shelter from contempt." Sixty-five years later the Oxford editor of Johnson remarked that these various observations on debtors "are such as would naturally suggest themselves to an honest and benevolent mind like Johnson's; but their political correctness may reasonably be questioned."

[49] *Works,* IV, 40. Boswell attributes this number to Bathurst, but L. F. Powell in "Johnson's Part in *The Adventurer*," *RES,* III (1927), 420–429, conclusively proves it to be Johnson's.
[50] *Works,* IV, 215, 263 .

Johnson's attitude on capital punishment was even more likely to be questioned, for it is the most progressive of his social notions. In *Rambler* No. 114 he argues on the grounds of utility though his deep compassion is apparent in every paragraph. In conclusion he says,

All laws against wickedness are ineffectual, unless some will inform, and some will prosecute; but till we mitigate the penalties for mere violations of property, information will always be hated, and prosecution dreaded. The heart of a good man cannot but recoil at the thought of punishing a slight injury with death; especially when he remembers that the thief might have procured safety by another crime, from which he was restrained only by his remaining virtue.

The obligations to assist the exercise of publick justice are indeed strong; but they will certainly be overpowered by tenderness for life. What is punished with severity contrary to our ideas of adequate retribution, will be seldom discovered; and multitudes will be suffered to advance from crime to crime, till they deserve death, because, if they had been sooner prosecuted, they would have suffered death before they deserved it.[51]

That Johnson in the last year of his life defended the public executions which seem to us so inhumane and lacking in solemn dignity, does not mean that he had retreated from his earlier position; he wished to preserve the monitory aspects of capital punishment, for he never doubted that it was justified in cases of murder. In fact, Johnson's substantial contribution to what was still a faltering cause did not come until 1777, when he gave his efforts and lent his great prestige in support of a man whose moral character was distasteful to him, Dr. William Dodd, who had been capitally convicted of forgery. In his *History of English Criminal Law: The Movement for Reform, 1750–1833* Leon Radzinowicz states that Dodd's case was "perhaps the first to stir the public conscience, and to force it to question whether the absolute capital punishment was socially and morally justifiable for all the offences for which it was then appointed." [52]

[51] *Works*, III, 43. See also *Works*, VI, 450 (King of Prussia).
[52] (New York, 1948), p. 451.

In his attitude toward capital punishment, as with the debtor's law, Johnson knew that he was premature and he shows it in *Rambler* No. 114. He admits that few seem willing to despair of the efficacy of capital inflictions and goes on to say that

of those who employ their speculations upon the present corruption of the people, some propose the introduction of more horrid, lingering, and terrifick punishments; some are inclined to accelerate the executions; some to discourage pardons; and all seem to think that lenity has given confidence to wickedness, and that we can only be rescued from the talons of robbery by inflexible rigour, and sanguinary justice.[53]

The first clause refers to extremists such as George Ollyffe, who in his *Essay Humbly Offer'd for an Act of Parliament to prevent Capital Crimes, and the Loss of many Lives, and to Promote a desirable Improvement and Blessing in the Nation* (1731) sought to make capital punishment more effective by introducing the methods of the torture chamber.

The remainder of Johnson's paragraph justly describes the views of most contemporary writers on criminology. For instance, it could refer to Henry Fielding, who is a good person to contrast with Johnson, since neither his public spirit nor his humaneness can be questioned. In *An Inquiry into the Causes of the late Increase of Robbers,* which came out the year before Johnson published this *Rambler,* Fielding, after first discussing the origin of crime from a sociological point of view and suggesting how it may be prevented, turns to criminal procedure and demands a stricter law of arrest, curtailment of the rights of the accused, severer punishments for certain crimes, a limitation on royal pardons, and more dignified executions. It is interesting to contrast his treatment of the reluctance of victims and witnesses to inform against culprits in capital cases, with that of the authoritarian and conservative Johnson which I have cited above:

As he is a good man, he should consider, that the principal duty which

---

[53] *Works,* III, 41.

every man owes, is to his country, for the safety and good of which all laws are established; and therefore his country requires of him to contribute all that in him lies to the due execution of those laws. Robbery is an offense not only against the party robbed, but against the public, who are therefore entitled to prosecution; and he who prevents or stifles such the prosecution, is no longer an innocent man, but guilty of a high offence against the public good.[54]

If Fielding seems severe today, especially when the latter part of his treatise is contrasted with Johnson's remarks, he did not seem so to the great majority of his contemporaries, for this is an extreme instance of that Johnsonian tendency, pointed out by Bronson, of swimming against the current. Public approval of capital punishment, supported by the authority of influential persons such as William Paley, continued strong throughout the century, and, although their effect was softened by increasing lenity in criminal procedure, laws were passed nearly every year creating new capital crimes, until finally in 1819 the number of such crimes, which had stood at 50 in 1688, is estimated to have been 223.[55]

A similar situation exists with respect to Johnson's best-known protest against a well-entrenched institution. Looking back we can distinguish foretokens of the doom of slavery and the slave trade as early as 1750. But these omens were not so easily detected by the average reader of the *Rambler*. Indeed, were he to adopt our deterministic perspective, to him the most portentious circumstance might seem to be the day-by-day increase of England's political and economic stake in the perpetuation of slavery, a process which was not reversed until the American Revolution.

The rapid increase of slaving by British ships actually began during Johnson's lifetime, after England obtained in 1713 by means of the now infamous, but then, acclaimed, *Asiento*, the right to import slaves into Spanish America. Sir Reginald Coupland estimates that by 1770 the number of slaves carried annually

---

[54] *Works*, edited by Arthur Murphy (1762), IV, 587.
[55] See Radzinowicz, pp. 4 and 37.

in British bottoms, had risen from five thousand in 1697 to fifty thousand. Even after the loss of the American colonies, thirty-eight thousand, the majority of those imported into the new world during 1787, were carried by British slavers.[56] It is easy to imagine how valuable this trade was to the merchant marine and to such cities as Liverpool and Bristol.

The importance to the British economy of slaveholding, as distinguished from slave trading, also increased rapidly during Johnson's day. And if the great economic benefits of this system were not attested by concrete evidence such as the prosperity of the slaving ports provided for the trade, the abuses of slaveholding were also conveniently hidden away in the West Indies, and were much less likely to come to the average Englishman's attention than the problems posed by foundlings or gin. Between 1690 and 1820 the slave population in Jamaica alone rose from forty thousand to three hundred and forty thousand, and it is some measure of the harshness of the system under which the slaves labored —British slavery was notably less humane than Spanish—that eight hundred thousand slaves had to be imported into the island during this period to bring about the increase.[57]

Of course, a literary tradition of protest against slavery and the trade existed long before Johnson came upon the scene, but a comparison of the poetical references to slavery by Defoe, Pope, Thomson, and Shenstone with Johnson's vigorous, bitter, and persistent denunciations confirms that he was the first major literary figure to become really concerned about the problem. Public sentiment did change enough during Johnson's lifetime so that some action was possible against slavery but not until his last decade. In 1774 the Quakers, who had for long led the only organized opposition, resolved to expel anyone who engaged in the trade, and in 1776 they enforced manumission by all Friends who still held slaves. Previously, in 1772, the seven-year struggle

[56] Reginald Coupland, *The British Anti-Slavery Movement* (1933), p. 22.
[57] Coupland, pp. 27 and 34.

of the first emancipator, Granville Sharp, had culminated in the freeing of all slaves in England and Ireland, and in 1778 a similar result was achieved for Scotland in the case of Joseph Knight, on which Johnson dictated an argument to Boswell. During these closing years of Johnson's life, the voices of John Wesley, Adam Smith, and many other influential men were raised against slavery, yet when Johnson died the Emancipation movement was still in its infancy.

When he first spoke out, and indeed for long after, he did so in opposition to the notions of a vast majority of his countrymen, who were either active proponents of slavery and the Trade, such as the shipping interests, elements in the Navy, and the powerful West Indian bloc, or who, though they might have no direct stake in it, felt, as Boswell did, that slavery was justified by precedent and necessitated by the sanctity of property, or who simply acquiesced in a system the real abuses of which could only be seen on the Gold Coast, on the Middle Passage or in the West Indies.

For many of Johnson's diatribes on slavery, motives can be found in his political allegiances at the particular time he wrote them, because during most of his life events placed him on the other side of the fence from those who had a vested interest in slavery. For instance, in 1740 it was natural enough for one associated with the opposition to attack Spain by means of a "Life of Drake." But a bitter sensitivity to injustice and inhumanity which reacts more profoundly than any partisan political loyalty, can be detected in his reference to Jamaica as "a place of great wealth and dreadful wickedness, a den of tyrants and a dungeon of slaves"; in the well-known query from *Taxation no Tyranny,* "how is it that we hear the loudest yelps for liberty among the drivers of negroes?" [58] and in the toast he once offered at Oxford, "Here's to the next insurrection of the negroes in the West Indies." [59] In fact, it is probable that the acrimony of those political

[58] *Works,* VI, 130 (Introduction to the Political State of Great Britain), 262.
[59] *Life,* III, 200.

tracts dealing with the Spanish, the West Indians, and the American colonists is especially intense because these three groups were so deeply involved with slavery.

That his bitterness toward these particular groups springs from something deeper than simple political partisanship is all the more credible, because Johnson associates slavery with the more general problem of the wholesale mistreatment of native populations by explorers and colonizers. Early in November of 1759, when all England was still rejoicing over the glorious news from Quebec, Johnson, in the guise of an Indian chief looking down on an English column, delivered the following history of the colonization of America: The

invaders ranged over the continent slaughtering, in their rage, those that resisted, and those that submitted, in their mirth. Of those that remained, some were buried in caverns, and condemned to dig metals for their masters; some were employed in tilling the ground, of which foreign tyrants devour the produce; and, when the sword and the mines have destroyed the natives, they supply their place by human beings of another colour, brought from some distant country to perish here under toil and torture.

But the chief sees the present war as an occasion for hope, a hope which might justify our calling Johnson a reactionary, but hardly a conservative:

But the time, perhaps, is now approaching, when the pride of usurpation shall be crushed, and the cruelties of invasion shall be revenged. The sons of rapacity have now drawn their swords upon each other, and referred their claims to the decision of war; let us look unconcerned upon the slaughter, and remember that the death of every European delivers the country from a tyrant and a robber; for what is the claim of either nation, but the claim of the vulture to the leveret, of the tiger to the fawn? . . . When they shall be weakened with mutual slaughter, let us rush down upon them, force their remains to take shelter in their ships, and reign once more in our native country.[60]

Greene derives an elaborate "theory of colonies" from Johnson's

---

[60] *Works*, IV, 389, 390–391 (*Idler* No. 81).

writings and proves conclusively that the key to it is "the position of the aboriginal inhabitants." [61]

Sometimes the indignation which Johnson directs against slave-owners and slave traders seems to derive from a conviction that they violate the natural rights of their victims. These are the only occasions on which he habitually resorts to this argument, which he belittles when others use it. As early as 1740, Johnson asserted the Negro's "natural right to liberty and independence" [62] and thirty-seven years later, when he argues the case of Joseph Knight, he is still asserting it:

It is said that, according to the constitutions of Jamaica, he was legally enslaved; these constitutions are merely positive; and apparently injurious to the rights of mankind, because whoever is exposed to sale is condemned to slavery without appeal. . . . No man is by nature the property of another: The defendant is, therefore, by nature free: The rights of nature must be some way forfeited before they can be justly taken away.[63]

Johnson's appeal to natural rights, however, is more of a justification of his stand than a motive for his assuming it in the first place. His real reasons are humanitarian as is clear from these remarks on the Portuguese explorers of Africa in his introduction to *The World Displayed* (1759):

They had the less scruple concerning their treatment of the savage people, because they scarcely considered them as distinct from beasts; and, indeed, the practice of all the European nations, and among others, of the English barbarians that cultivate the southern islands of America, proves, that this opinion, however absurd and foolish, however wicked and injurious, still continues to prevail.[64]

In part, inhumanity consists of not recognizing and respecting the humanity of others.

I have emphasized the timing of Johnson's biting commentary

[61] *Politics,* pp. 165–172.
[62] *Works,* VI, 313 (Drake).
[63] *Life,* III, 202–203.
[64] *Works,* V, 218.

on some contemporary institutions because if the timing is ignored, as it commonly is, it is possible completely to overlook the truth that these are emphatically not the views of a man who reveres precedent, authority, and stability above all else. If we consider when they were spoken, we cannot look on them as transient aberrations in the conduct of a man with an inveterately conservative turn of mind. It is certainly closer to the mark to regard his attitude on debtors, on capital punishment, and on slavery as the result of a victory by his greatheartedness over his inherent conservatism, but this answer will not suffice for our purposes. Although it is always best, all things being equal, to embrace the simplest solution, this fashion of reducing a mind to a few neat ambivalences is altogether too simple to do justice to Johnson's remarkably rich and varied consciousness. Greene's discussion of Johnson's humanitarian tendencies represents a further advance because it makes clear how thoroughly they pervade his thinking on many subjects, but since Greene must properly concentrate on politics, he is content to ascribe these tendencies to early religious influences. Whatever their ultimate spring—at this stage Johnson's explicit ideas interest us more than his fundamental motives do—Johnson's social and economic utterances, like his political statements, do not proceed directly from any overflow of emotion, religious or otherwise, their immediate source is a rather orderly body of notions, to which we must now turn.

ℰ v ℈

Social Theory and Moral Practice

We can get a glimpse of the moral framework which underlies Johnson's social utterances by examining his diverse attitudes toward riches and the rich. These attitudes can be distinguished on the basis of whether they refer to the getting of riches or to the proper use of them. On the former subject he is especially outspoken. Few books have ever been recommended to prospective purchasers by a stranger preface than the one Johnson wrote for John Payne's *New Tables of Interest* (1758). After stating that the tables were principally designed for stockbrokers and proprietors of the public funds and after admitting that among the former there are "men of great honour and probity, who are candid and open in all their transactions," he laments that their profession should be brought into discredit by

the intrusion of bad men, who, instead of serving their country, and procuring an honest subsistence in the army or the fleet, endeavour to maintain luxurious tables, and splendid equipages, by sporting with the public credit.

He warns them against any return to the stockjobbing of yore and admonishes them to take steps against any

desperate sons of fortune, who, not having the courage of highwaymen take 'Change-alley rather than the road, because, though more injurious than highwaymen, they are less in danger of punishment by the loss either of liberty or life.

For the other patrons, the proprietors of the public funds, he has but one stern sentence:

No motive can sanctify the accumulation of wealth, but an ardent desire to make the most honorable and virtuous use of it, by contributing to the support of good government, the increase of arts and industry, the rewards of genius and virtue, and the relief of wretchedness and want.[1]

Johnson may have done his old friend a disservice by these sentiments, but if he did so the fault was in part Payne's for choosing him to write the preface, since he merely said what in more appropriate contexts he had said before and was to say again and again thereafter.

There is nothing essentially wrong about acquiring wealth. Even early in his literary career, Johnson was not "certain, that the accumulation of honest gain ought to be hindered. . . . Whatever can enable the possessor to confer any benefit upon others, may be desired upon virtuous principles."[2] The trouble is that wealth is seldom desired on virtuous principles and he who does desire it on them is not likely to get it. Johnson's mistrust of the acquisition of wealth arises from the basic contradiction involved; the motive which is most successful in impelling men to accumulate a great fortune is that which is least likely to promote virtuous use of it, avarice. Thus the remark of Johnson's recalled by

---

[1] *Works,* V, 450–451. I fail to see that Johnson here "rises to the defense of stockbrokers," as Greene suggests in his *Politics,* p. 240. Considering the context, Johnson's one favorable remark in the preface, his admission that "among brokers of stock are men of great honour and probity," is faint praise indeed.

[2] *Works,* IV, 116 (*Adventurer* No. 119).

Strahan that "there are few ways in which a man can be more innocently employed than in getting money" is not typical. As Johnson matures, he no longer speaks in the caustically indignant tones of his youthful period:

> The Lust of Gold succeeds the Rage of Conquest
> The Lust of Gold, unfeeling and Remorseless!
> The last Corruption of degenerate Man! [3]

But many years after *Irene* was written he is saying the same thing in substance,

> As there is no desire so extensive, or so continual in its exertions, that possesses so many minds, or operates with such resistless activity; there is none that deviates into greater irregularity, or more frequently corrupts the heart of man, than the wish to enlarge possession and accumulate wealth. [4]

Getting money can mean corruption for the individual, harm to others, and no ultimate benefit to society.

Accordingly, from one point of view, that which regards the getting of it, wealth must be considered only a relative good. For example, if in amassing riches a man injures "widows and orphans," to use Johnson's phrase, this injury must be weighed in the balance whenever any good the man accomplishes with his money is assessed. However, Johnson considers wealth in itself as a positive good, and he stigmatizes as cant the remarks of those who say otherwise. Riches are good because the spending of them benefits the economic structure and because, from a social point of view, they enable their possessor to relieve want and distress.

I think that if these distinctions are kept in mind most of that apparent ambiguity in Johnson's attitude towards the world of

---

[3] *Poems*, p. 249 (*Irene* I, i, 13–15).

[4] *Works*, IX, 453 (Sermon XVIII). See, for example, *Rambler* No. 131; *Works*, VI, 136 (The Political State of Great Britain); *Works*, VI, 228 (*Taxation no Tyranny*); Sermon IV; *Works*, IX, 345–346 (Sermon VI); and *Works*, IX, 455 (Sermon XVIII).

trade and commerce which some scholars have remarked can be resolved. On going through one of those traditional compilations of Johnson's sayings on various topics, we might well find all his pronouncements upon some morally indifferent matter—tea drinking, for instance—to be perfectly consistent, and we would certainly find uniformity at the other extreme where the moral issues are incontrovertible—on the subject, say, of Hobbism—but we have no reason whatsoever to expect any uniformity of attitude regarding a number of subjects which lie between these extremes. Especially is this true with respect to anything with so many complex practical ramifications as what we now call "business." Indeed it would be rather astonishing were we to find that he always felt the same toward merchants *qua* merchants or toward commerce as a whole, for in anything which bears upon life it is the moral consequences which are crucial to Johnson, and these vary greatly for different phases of commerce and with different practitioners. The truth of this is borne out, for instance, by John H. Middendorf's illuminating study "Dr. Johnson and Mercantilism," [5] in which he concludes that where Johnson disagrees with this prevailing economic theory of his times, he usually does so on grounds which are ultimately moral. If we consider each of his judgments upon commerce as an individual case and keep in mind that, although Johnson regards wealth as a positive good, he usually judges the amassing or spending of it with respect to the impact these processes have upon men as individuals, we will find little ambiguity.

It may come as a surprise that one who so often says that the chief purpose of getting money is to help others, at the same time defends expending it self-indulgently upon luxuries. Of course, the context in which such remarks occur must be taken into consideration. In all contexts, he vigorously expounds the duty of charity. The public benefits of self-indulgence are not pointed out in the *Sermons,* for instance; such notions are largely confined to

[5] *JHI,* XXI (1960), 66–83.

his private conversations. Nevertheless, when he does defend luxury, there is no doubting his sincerity, or his debt to Bernard Mandeville, despite his denial of the obligation when Miss Seward points it out to him.[6] Perhaps he denies the debt because he does not wish to be thought of as defending private vices, and, furthermore, as he goes on to say, Mandeville is too much a puritan, for neither is all wealth socially beneficial nor all pleasure, vicious.

Typical of his arguments on this subject are the remarks he makes to George Steevens and Boswell one morning in 1776:

Now the truth is, that luxury produces much good. Take the luxury of building in London. Does it not produce real advantage in the conveniency and elegance of accomodation, and this all from the exertion of industry? People will tell you, with a melancholy face, how many builders are in gaol. It is plain that they are in gaol, not for building; for rents are not fallen.—A man gives half a guinea for a dish of green peas. How much gardening does this occasion? how many labourers must the competition to have such things early in the market, keep in employment? [7]

On this occasion he goes on to maintain as he does elsewhere sometimes,[8] that money spent on luxury may well do more good than that given directly from benevolent motives:

You will hear it said, very gravely, "Why, was not the half-guinea, thus spent in luxury, not given to the poor? To how many might it have afforded a good meal?" Alas! has it not gone to the *industrious* poor, whom it is better to support than the *idle* poor? You are much surer that you are doing good when you *pay* money to those who work, as the recompence of their labour, than when you *give* money merely in charity.

---

[6] *Life*, III, 291–292. Because the chief purpose of Earl R. Miner's perceptive article on "Dr. Johnson, Mandeville, and 'Publick Benefits,' " in *HLQ*, XXI (1958), 159–166, is to correct the traditional misconception that Johnson appropriated Mandeville's credo in toto, its author does not precisely define the area of agreement between these men who were both pessimists and both utilitarians. Johnson would restate Mandeville's thesis in the form "Private luxury often produces public benefits."

[7] *Life*, III, 55–56.

[8] See also, for instance, *Life*, IV, 173.

Unlike many of his fellow altruists Johnson was well aware of the pitfalls involved in direct charity. These Mandevillian sentiments are also due in part to his utilitarian bent and to his strong feeling for society as an organic whole, all strata of which are interdependent, but there is no evidence that, on a practical level, he himself followed Mandeville's theory.

Johnson usually argues that luxury promotes the welfare of society, and he sometimes tends to ignore that of the individual chiefly concerned:

As to the rout that is made about people who are ruined by extravagance, it is no matter to the nation that some individuals suffer. When so much general productive exertion is the consequence of luxury, the nation does not care though there are debtors in gaol; nay, they would not care though their creditors were there too.[9]

The thesis is Cumberland's, that is good which produces the greatest happiness for the greatest number.[10]

As I have said, it will not do for Johnson to preach private ruination as public service, and when he is moralizing, economic theory is forgotten, and the duty of direct charity becomes his theme. Charity is the subject of several fervent sermons, a number of *Ramblers* and *Idlers* are devoted to it, and the briefer references to this duty spread through Johnson's writings and conversation are almost innumerable. A typical exhortation from the *Sermons* will serve to illustrate these because, if it is more impassioned than many of his injunctions regarding charity, it reveals all the more clearly the intensity of conviction which underlies all of them. In answer to his own question as to how a man "shall hinder his wealth from flying away, and leaving him nothing but melancholy, disappointment, and remorse"—a process he himself has graphically described in several places—he replies,

This he can effect only by the practice of charity, by dealing his bread to the hungry, and bringing the poor that is cast out to his house. . . .

[9] *Life*, III, 56.
[10] *The Laws of Nature*, pp. 21–22.

By a liberal distribution of his riches, he can place them above the reach of the spoiler, and exempt them from accident and danger; can purchase to himself that satisfaction which no power on earth can take away; and make them the means of happiness, when they are no longer in his hands. He may procure, by this means of his wealth, what he will find to be obtained by no other method of applying it, an alleviation of the sorrows of age, of the pains of sickness, and of the agonies of death.[11]

Johnson's remarks on poverty and the poor tend to confirm these insights into his social notions offered by his commentary on wealth. In the first place, if riches are a positive good, poverty is positively evil. His reply to Soame Jenyns's cant upon the subject is well known; *Rambler* No. 202 is just as pungent:

But it will be found upon a nearer view, that they who extol the happiness of poverty, do not mean the same state with those who deplore its miseries. . . . He that wishes to become a philosopher at a cheap rate, easily gratifies his ambition by submitting to poverty, when he does not feel it, and by boasting his contempt of riches when he has already more than he enjoys.[12]

With the bitterness of one who had felt them, Johnson goes on to point out that, in addition to real suffering, ignominy and contempt are the lot of the poor, and he quotes Hooker to the effect that poverty is "such an impediment to virtue, as, till it be removed, suffreth not the mind of man to admit any other care."

However distressed, the victims of poverty are not exempt from the obligation of charity, for charity

is an universal duty, which it is in every man's power sometimes to practise; since every degree of assistance given to another, upon proper motives, is an act of charity; and there is scarcely any man, in such a state of imbecility, as that he may not, on some occasions, benefit his neighbour. He that cannot relieve the poor may instruct the ignorant; and he that cannot attend the sick may reclaim the vitious.[13]

[11] *Works*, IX, 323–324 (Sermon IV).
[12] *Works*, III, 437–438.
[13] *Works*, IX, 325 (Sermon IV).

Nevertheless, Johnson admits that one of poverty's chief evils is that it deprives its victims of the power of directly doing good. He uses this as an argument in admonishing Boswell on the danger of going too far into debt:

Consider a man whose fortune is very narrow; whatever be his rank by birth, or whatever his reputation by intellectual excellence, what good can he do? or what evil can he prevent? That he cannot help the needy is evident, he has nothing to spare. But, perhaps, his advice or admonition may be useful. His poverty will destroy his influence: many more can find that he is poor, than that he is wise; and few will reverence the understanding that is of so little advantage to its owner. . . . Of riches, it is not necessary to write the praise. Let it, however, be remembered, that he who has money to spare, has it always in his power to benefit others; and of such power a good man must always be desirous.[14]

Were their contribution restricted to direct charity, the moral function of the poorer classes in a society where how much one benefits others is the measure of merit would be small indeed. Yet, humbler folk do have an indirect function analogous to that served by the rich when, by simply spending money on luxuries, they give aid to others; only, among these lower classes it is the major contribution, not a subsidiary one. Typical of an idea which recurs constantly in Johnson's more didactic writings are his remarks in *Adventurer* No. 67:

When I look around upon those who are . . . variously exerting their qualifications, I cannot but admire the secret concatenation of society that links together the great and the mean, the illustrious and the obscure; and consider with benevolent satisfaction, that no man, unless his body or mind be totally disabled, has need to suffer the mortification of seeing himself useless or burthensome to the community: he that will diligently labour, in whatever occupation, will deserve the sustenance which he obtains, and the protection which he enjoys; and may lie down every night with the pleasing consciousness of having contributed something to the happiness of life.[15]

[14] *Letters*, II, 486 (3 June, 1782).
[15] *Works*, IV, 43.

That they fail to make this sort of contribution is still another reason why Johnson disapproves of recluses. We noted earlier that the recluse wilfully circumscribes his possible field of moral action; he may fulfill his duty to God and to himself, but not to others. And Johnson seems just as concerned that the cloistered man evades his share of the world's work, indirect beneficence, as he is that the recluse shuns the moral crises which the man of the world continually encounters and shirks the obligation of direct beneficence which the latter must discharge. Thus, in regard to Cowley we should "let neither our reverence for a genius, nor our pity for a sufferer, dispose us to forget that, if his activity was virtue, his retreat was cowardice." [16] In *Idler* No. 19 he expands upon the theme:

To the scheme of these solitary speculatists, it has been justly objected that if they are happy, they are happy only by being useless. That mankind is one vast republick, where every individual receives many benefits from the labours of others, which, by labouring in his turn for others, he is obliged to repay; and that where the united efforts of all are not able to exempt all from misery, none have a right to withdraw from their task of vigilance, or to be indulged in idle wisdom or solitary pleasures. [17]

According to these principles, any sort of extended idleness is immoral because anyone who shirks his duty of being immediately useful also fails to be indirectly altruistic.

In the midst of this universal hurry, no man ought to be so little influenced by example, or so void of honest emulation, as to stand a lazy spectator of incessant labour; or please himself with the mean happiness of a drone, while active swarms are buzzing about him: no man is without some quality, by the due application of which he might deserve well of the world; and whoever he be that has but little in his power, should be in haste to do that little, lest he be confounded with him that can do nothing. [18]

[16] *Lives*, I, 10.
[17] *Works*, IV, 204. See also *Works*, IX, 313.
[18] *Works*, IV, 43–44 (*Adventurer* No. 67).

It is significant that Johnson's most forceful discussions of this subject were written in his later forties after he had completed the *Dictionary* and, having accepted subscriptions for his edition of Shakespeare, declined into what seemed to him incurable indolence. His always poignant awareness of the night that cometh served not to prod him on, but to deepen his misery—even the title of the *Idler* is self-reproaching—and frequent among his meditations are prayers such as this:

Impress upon my soul such repentance of the days mispent in idleness and folly, that I may, henceforward, diligently attend to the business of my station in this world, and to all the duties which thou hast commanded. . . . Let my life be useful, and my death be happy.[19]

Because this urgent concern with work and activity is a fundamental moral impulse in Johnson, because it is more relevant to the why of moral conduct than to the problem of what moral conduct is, it is better analyzed later when we will be dealing with the motives to morality. For our present purposes it is enough to note that Johnson insists that the rich, the poor, the artist, the statesman, and the artisan—all men—must make the most of whatever abilities have been allotted them, and that he justifies this insistence on the utilitarian and altruistic grounds, that all can and must contribute to the general happiness and prosperity, that even the humblest effort, when considered from the economic standpoint, has utility and, having utility, is from the social standpoint, altruistic.

Johnson's doctrine of subordination is best appraised in connection with the social and economic ideas we have been considering. In fact, to evaluate the doctrine separately from them is to wrench it out of context. We have seen that Johnson justifies political subordination on the grounds of utility; both utilitarian and altruistic principles are responsible for his attitude toward the sort of subordination which is largely social and economic in nature.

[19] *Works,* IX, 215 (*Prayers and Meditations,* Sept. 18, 1758).

It is true that Johnson does not attempt to defend the process by which social and economic distinctions arise, as he does in the case of political subordination. Rather, he tends to accept these distinctions as given, as a necessary premise if one is to discuss the social organism, and then he proceeds to justify their existence. Any specific ordering produced by social and economic forces may involve many anomalies, yet some sort of subordination is not only inevitable but desirable. The prime cause of social subordination lies in the natural inequality of men. "So far is it from being true that men are naturally equal, that no two people can be half an hour together, but one shall acquire an evident superiority over the other." [20]

Economically considered, subordination is also inevitable, because there are not enough goods to go around.

It must necessarily happen, that many will desire what few can possess, and consequently, that some will be fortunate by the disappointment, or defeat, of others, and, since no man suffers disappointment without pain, that one must become miserable by another's happiness. This is, however, the natural condition of human life.[21]

Toward this economic subordination Johnson is much less deferential than he is toward that which is based on rank and birth. In rebutting the harsh and inflexible system of subordination propounded by Soame Jenyns, Johnson does find something to praise in the incessant flux of status common to mercantile nations:

To entail irreversible poverty upon generation after generation, only because the ancestor happened to be poor, is, in itself, cruel, if not unjust, and is contrary to the maxims of a commercial nation, which always suppose and promote a rotation of property, and offer every individual a chance of mending his condition by his diligence.[22]

But more often, especially in his later years, Johnson is suspicious

[20] *Life*, II, 13.
[21] *Works*, IX, 497 (Sermon XXIII). See also Greene's *Politics*, p. 195.
[22] *Works*, VI, 56–57.

of the distinctions which arise from wealth. After maintaining "the dignity and propriety of male succession" for ancient estates, in opposition to the opinion of Bennet Langton, he goes on to say, "as for an estate newly acquired by trade, you may give it, if you will, to the dog *Towser* and let him keep his *own* name." [23]

Johnson's observation of feudal life in the Hebrides confirmed him in the opinion that money confounds true subordination, and that distinctions based principally on wealth contravert the purpose of this true subordination since they are the product of the very sort of strife which social distinctions are intended to suppress. A real advantage of any system of hereditary subordination is that it results at any given moment in distinctions which are purely arbitrary and which are therefore less open to question than those distinctions arising from systems or processes based on fitness or merit. As he once put it to Boswell, "Sir, there would be a perpetual struggle for precedence, were there no fixed invariable rules for the distinction of rank, which creates no jealousy, as it is allowed to be accidental." [24]

Thus, there is considerable justification for the complaint that Johnson dogmatically insists on the acceptance of arbitrary social distinctions. What is unjust, however, is to interpret subordination, in the sense Johnson uses the word, as mere stratification. Such an interpretation completely ignores the fact that Johnson always considers society as an organism and continually argues for human solidarity within that whole. The natural inequality of mankind may be the cause of subordination, but utility is its justification.

Within a society conceived organically, subordination means something more than power on one hand and subjection on the other. It presupposes among all ranks duty and responsibility as well as rights and privileges, mutual interdependence, in place of some human equivalent of that pecking order which flourishes in

[23] *Life,* II, 261.
[24] *Life,* I, 448. See also I, 442.

every chicken coop. Johnson far more frequently concerns himself with duty than with privilege. In Sermon I after observing how the family of mankind is divided and subdivided into particular communities and associations, he goes on to say that

each of these subdivisions produces new dependencies and relations, and every particular relation gives rise to a particular scheme of duties. Duties which are of the utmost importance, and of the most sacred obligation, as the neglect of them would defeat all the blessings of society, and cut off even the hope of happiness; as it would poison the fountain whence it must be drawn, and make those institutions, which have been formed as necessary to peace and satisfaction, the means of disquiet and misery.[25]

As we have seen, in such an organism even the humblest, if he is directly benevolent and if he works to the best of his abilities, can contribute to happiness and is justified in feeling that he serves society's ultimate purposes.

This is a simple idea indeed and certainly a commonplace one among Johnson's contemporaries. For instance, he has no real quarrel with the general outlines of Soame Jenyns's social theory; it is too close to his own. Even a brief discussion of the concept would hardly be justified, were it not that the impact of nineteenth-century liberalism and *laissez-faire* economics has left a few of Johnson's critics blind to the concept's implications. The fact that these same critics seldom show awareness of Johnson's strong feeling for human solidarity illustrates this point. His compassion for his fellow men is apparent to all, but this compassion is a sufficient motive only for his personal charity. Informing his idea of an organic, mutually interdependent subordination is a more complex spirit which in its simplest form is bred of the awareness that in a marginal economy there must always be those without sufficient food and shelter, and that only by united effort incessantly applied can men drive back the spectre of want. The degree to which sloth and gluttony no longer seem so deadly as

[25] *Works,* IX, 290.

the other five sins, is the measure of our prosperity and also of how much we have lost this simple solidarity, even though we are in reality more dependent upon each other than ever before. In its more complex phase this spirit of solidarity, like that preached by Joseph Conrad, derives from an awareness of the tragedy of human existence and of the more comprehensive evil surrounding man, which cannot be successfully faced alone.

This spirit, a cause rather than an effect of his compassion, gives the real meaning to Johnson's conviction that "no man is born merely for his own sake," that

every man is obliged by the Supreme Master of the universe to improve all the opportunities of good which are afforded him, and to keep in continual activity such abilities as are bestowed on him. But he has no reason to repine, though his abilities are small and his opportunities few,[26]

for

whoever steadily perseveres in the exertion of all his faculties, does what is great with respect to himself; and what will not be despised by Him, who has given all created beings their different abilities; he faithfully performs the task of life, within whatever limits his labours may be confined, or how soon soever they may be forgotten.[27]

As was the case with many of his specific political doctrines, some of Johnson's social and economic principles can be illustrated from Richard Cumberland's *De legibus naturae,* and in this instance we can feel fairly confident that this treatise is the ultimate source of Johnson's particular concept of the moral purposes of the social organism, because Cumberland was the first to propound such a blend of altruistic and utilitarian purposes for society.

Even in those social and economic notions which were certainly not original with Cumberland the parallel is marked. Compare his remarks on the purposes of subordination with those of Johnson just cited:

[26] *Works,* IV, 411 (*Idler* No. 88).
[27] *Works,* IV, 132 (*Adventurer* No. 128).

It is *evident,* "That the procuring the greatest Good the whole Society of Rational Beings is capable of, . . . depends necessarily upon the concurrent Assistance of *every one,* by mutual Services of very different Kinds," *and* That it is therefore impossible to obtain such Effect, tho' foreseen and design'd, with *Certainty* and *Steddiness,* except a *Subordination of Rational Beings* be establish'd.[28]

Cumberland assures the humbler orders of their importance to the social organism, using the same argument which occurs so frequently in Johnson:

It is very well known, that they who have *least in their power,* benefit others; either by the *Exchange* of Things or Services, or by *observing Compacts,* or by giving us reason to place a Confidence in them, even without Compacts, or by the *Examples* which they afford (if not of great Exploits, yet) of *Industry, Patience* or *Innocence.* . . . I own, however, that the *Advantage* is *but small,* which each receives from many, especially the *more remote,* but we give them in *return* only a *like share* of the effects of our Industry; yet even *these cannot with safety be neglected,* because the *whole Happiness,* and that not small, of particular Persons, grows out of such *minute* offices of Humanity included in the care of the Common Good, almost in the same manner *as* this most beautiful *Frame* of the Material *World* arises, from the regular Motions and Figures of the *minute* Particles of Matter.[29]

Social philosophers have from the first conceived of the state as a cooperative effort for the common good, many of them have insisted that its structure must be truly organic, not merely hierarchical, and not a few have defined social duty in terms of love and work, direct charity and indirect utility. The distinctive feature of the social theory of Cumberland and his followers is the intensely practical, utilitarian end for which the organism is set up and which the performance of social duty is intended to achieve.

Although we do not know how he would feel about being called a member of the school of Cumberland, Johnson did adopt

---

[28] *The Laws of Nature,* p. 348. The original is more specific as to the meaning of "subordination": *nisi rationalium alii aliis perpetua serie subordinentur* (1672), p. 384.

[29] *The Laws of Nature,* p. 236.

this distinctive utilitarian ideal. For him the common good is not an abstraction; it consists of the sum of the various happinesses of the particular individuals who make up a society. As with his political notions, Johnson's aim is not to serve some principle but to achieve a practical result. Of course, to specify the happiness of particular individuals is to speak in terms only slightly less vague and abstract than the "general happiness" of "common good" usually spoken of by social philosophers—unless, that is, this individual happiness is defined. Johnson defines it precisely enough in negative terms, and here his pessimism helps us—his clear insight into the unhappiness, the misfortune, the evil, about him, and his unshakeable conviction of their reality and inevitability. When he is speaking in social and economic contexts, Johnson means by *happiness,* merely the achieving of certain minimal goods and the avoidance of misery.

When we look upon his political and social theories together from this negative point of view, and especially when we give proper emphasis to the extremely practical character of the ends Johnson is seeking in both, it becomes obvious that there is no real inconsistency between his political and social aims, that *Taxation no Tyranny* and the fervid and dissident criticism of imprisonment for debt in *Idler* No. 38 flow naturally from the same pen. Ascribing them to Johnson's separate conservative and humanitarian impulses possesses the virtue of simplicity and the vice of half truth.

Consider his stricture upon the American colonists: "If slavery be thus fatally contagious, how is it that we hear the loudest yelps for liberty among the drivers of negroes?" The irony here goes beyond the idea that the Americans while demanding one form of liberty are denying another form to the negroes. It depends on the conviction that the liberty which the Americans demand is abstract, not real and tangible, that, granting his pessimistic attitude regarding all types of government, the Americans have about all the liberty anyone has a right to expect; whereas, one would have to expect much less efficiency from the economic and social machinery than even Johnson does, to deny that the slaves suffer real misery indeed, as a result of the loss of their fundamental rights.

The practical aim which he proposes for political society has been remarked by many students of Johnson. It is typified in his declaration that "all that is to be valued, or indeed can be enjoyed by individuals, is *private* liberty. Political liberty is good only so far as it produces private liberty." [30] His economic and social aims are just as utilitarian. In every case where Johnson is moved to vigorous protest against the institutions of his day there is some very tangible evil which he seeks to alleviate, whether it be the wretchedness of servitude, the agonies of the imprisoned debtor and the destitution suffered by his family, or the terrors of those condemned to death, often for some trivial offense. His social aims are the product of a strenuously practical mind operating upon the stuff and substance of his earlier days in London, the poverty, vice, sickness, and squalor which he daily encountered. And if Johnson's aims seem circumscribed by a pessimism bred in part by this early experience, that same experience gives force and conviction to his humanitarian utterances and preserves him from those follies which sometimes afflict more optimistic humanitarians.

Practical benefit unites all phases of Johnson's concept of society. The political, economic, and social organisms are intended to give the mass of individuals certain fundamental benefits—not a guarantee of happiness, but those things without which happiness is impossible. The ultimate end of political institutions "is to secure private happiness from private malignity, to keep individuals from the power of one another." Once the political institutions have secured for the individual this limited freedom of action, this "peace" as Johnson frequently calls it, the social and economic structure ought ideally to provide him with a niche

[30] *Life*, II, 60.

where he can earn at least the essentials required to maintain life and at the same time fulfill his responsibility of beneficence, if not through direct charity, then indirectly through his contribution to the system as a whole. No man can with easy conscience remain idle while the organism fails, as usually it must, in achieving these minimum ends.

The scope of these benefits which society can provide and which all its members ought to promote, is limited at the top of the scale by Johnson's pessimism. Political institutions are human institutions, and can be no better than the imperfect beings through which they function. The economic structure also suffers from this liability, and, in addition is hampered by unavoidable inefficiencies of production and distribution and is, further, subject to the whims of nature. But there is also a bottom limit, defined by Johnson's moral impulses, his humanity, and his intransigence when confronted with evil.

I suspect that one of the chief reasons why Johnson has been charged with contradicting himself is that his later political tracts reveal very little of that deep sympathy for the lower orders which is so evident when he writes on social problems. Against his pleas on behalf of slaves and criminals can be weighed such a passage as this one from *The False Alarm,* where a man of rank exhorts a circulator of petitions that, instead, he ought to be telling the people

that submission is the duty of the ignorant, and content the virtue of the poor; that they have no skill in the art of government, nor any interest in the dissensions of the great; and when you meet with any, as some there are, whose understandings are capable of conviction, it will become you to allay this foaming ebullition, by showing them, that they have as much happiness as the condition of life will easily receive.[31]

A similarly contemptuous tone is evident in *The Patriot* where the lower classes, personified as the weak, the ignorant, the credu-

[31] *Works,* VI, 174.

lous, and the mean—are "base and gross and profligate." The example of Johnson's brief political sympathy with the populace during his youth makes it even more tempting to ascribe these divergent tones of his later years, compassionate and contemptuous, to contradictory impulses in his personality.

Mrs. Catherine Macaulay, too "wondered how he could reconcile his political principles with his moral; his notions of inequality and subordination with wishing well to the happiness of all mankind." [32] But it is easy enough to reconcile them and we need not resort to divergent aspects of Johnson's character, for the real divergence is between him and Mrs. Macaulay, between his habit of thought and that of his critics. She does not accept inequality, and the happiness and equality she talks about are abstract and theoretical, a fact which Johnson pointed up by inviting her footman to sit down at the dinner table. He considers inequality axiomatic and he feels that individual happiness depends in the first place on fundamental, concrete pleasures and upon the absence of misery. If inequality is accepted as a fact, it follows in Johnson's way of thinking that the best way to secure this happiness is through some general scheme of subordination. All may have an equal right, as far as the economy permits, to those things without which happiness is impossible, but this is not to say that all men are equally qualified to direct the course of society in the pursuit of that happiness, or that, even if they were, it would be wise to let them all try it at once.

There is also a quantitative aspect of social good. He seeks the happiness, not, perhaps, of all, as Mrs. Macaulay put it, but, at least, of the greatest possible number. Accordingly, the abuses which Johnson attacks most vigorously, slavery, imprisonment for debt, and indiscriminate application of the death penalty, affect directly or indirectly large numbers of people, as he continually reminds his readers. And for a similar reason Johnson habitually attempts to determine the total amounts of good and evil, happi-

[32] *Life*, II, 219.

ness and misery, which result from an action before pronouncing it virtuous or vicious. Here again he agrees with Soame Jenyns, who is confident that we are enabled not only to determine which are good, and which are evil actions, "but, almost mathematically, to demonstrate the proportion of virtue or vice which belongs to each, by comparing them with the degrees of happiness or misery which they occasion." [33]

Johnson does recognize that such determinations are not easy to make,[34] and he is certainly aware that all pleasures are not of equal value, but he never faces up to some of the implications of this quantitative interpretation of the common good. His unquestioning acceptance of the political principle that it is better for a few to suffer misery and injustice than to disturb the peace of many—which has understandably distressed some critics—is easy enough to rationalize on utilitarian principles. Circumstance will decide whom is to be thrown out of the sleigh, which the wolves must overtake unless it is lightened, and "whom?" is the only problem, since the necessity for doing something cannot be questioned. To balance a small evil against the possibility of a much greater catastrophe is easily done, but it is not easy to poise good against evil when they are more nearly equal in magnitude, to decide whether a certain quantum of happiness justifies the concomitant misery. However, Johnson is a moralist not a social philosopher; his rule does have many practical applications and we cannot expect him to resolve all the problems inherent in the utilitarian thesis.

When we consider the fundamental principles underlying Johnson's notions, his feeling that the goal of the social and political organism is the greatest possible quantity of individual happiness among its members and that this goal is best attained by direct and indirect beneficence among these members, by love and work, it is apparent that his is a practical version of the utilitarian credo

---

[33] *Works,* VI, 68 (Review of a *Free Enquiry*).
[34] *Works,* VI, 71–72 (Review of a *Free Enquiry*).

which was first stated by Cumberland. Cumberland phrased his law of nature as follows:

The greatest Benevolence of every rational Agent towards all, forms the happiest State of every, and of all the Benevolent, as far as is in their Power; and is necessarily requisite to the happiest State which they can attain, and therefore the common Good is the supreme law.[35]

The chief difference between this general statement and the principles which underly Johnson's social ethic is the more practical nature of the latter. Johnson never forgets that if the organism as a whole is to function and if the individual is to have the opportunity to be directly beneficent, social duty must consist in a balance of attention to one's own everyday concerns and to the needs of others. Benevolence embraces work and prudence as well as love.

This statement tends to emphasize the utilitarian end of social duty rather than its altruistic motive. Any doubts concerning the importance of altruism in Johnson's social thinking can be dispelled by considering what the duty of the individual is toward those who are not a part of the particular organism to which he belongs, duty which cannot result in any increase in the total happiness of society. If beneficence were merely a means to utility, one would expect its obligation to cease in instances where no utility could be produced; on the contrary the duty of beneficence extends to all men.

Johnson is fond of the notion that the great society of the world is divided

into different communities, which are again divided into smaller bodies, and more contracted associations, which pursue, or ought to pursue, a particular interest, in subordination to the publick good, and consistently with the general happiness of mankind.[36]

Therefore, it is not always apparent what specific community Johnson intends when he refers to the individual's contribution

[35] *The Laws of Nature,* p. 41.
[36] *Works,* IX, 290 (Sermon I).

to the whole, as he does in this passage from *Adventurer* No. 137.

The business of life is carried on by a general co-operation; in which the part of any single man can be no more distinguished, than the effect of a particular drop when the meadows are floated by a summer shower: yet every drop increases the inundation, and every hand adds to the happiness or misery of mankind.[37]

Most of the time he is thinking of England, often of Great Britain, and occasionally he includes the English possessions overseas. The political and economic organism of which he speaks lies within these borders and his sociological thinking usually has a similarly restricted area of reference. This community then is the largest unit in which he normally thinks of the utilitarian principle as operating effectively.

In theory, however, the obligation of beneficence extends beyond this realm and beyond the limit of utility to include all mankind. Even though he seldom has an opportunity, as he did when he criticized Portuguese and Spanish explorers, to point out specific application for this broader rule, he commonly phrases his altruistic precepts in a universally applicable form. Thus, in his moral writings there continually recur phrases such as "the great republic of mankind," "the universal league of social beings," "the great law of mutual benevolence"; and similar expressions. These phrases represent an application of the Christian precept of universal love, yet something more is involved: Johnson's firm conviction, in the face of a growing relativism, that universality confers validity. Perhaps there is also some influence of a concept which found new life and increasing vigor in the eighteenth century, the old, ultimately Stoic, notion of universal brotherhood, the same idea which inspired the third Earl of Shaftesbury to exclaim, in the privacy of his diary, "I am a citizen of the world."

Johnson is more practical than Shaftesbury, to be sure, and although the law of mutual benevolence is universally applicable

[37] *Works*, IV, 141.

and is the fundamental maxim of all societies, he has no great faith in its widespread application.

To love all men is our duty, so far as it includes a general habit of benevolence, and readiness of occasional kindness; but to love all equally is impossible; at least impossible without the extinction of those passions which now produce all our pains and all our pleasures; without the disuse, if not the abolition, of some of our faculties, and the suppression of all our hopes and fears in apathy and indifference.[38]

Because general benevolence is not efficacious, "the great community of mankind is . . . necessarily broken into smaller independent societies" and these are in turn subdivided. The smaller the social unit involved, the more efficient will be the altruistic motive. The universal obligation does exist, but the gap between the ideal and the possibility of fulfillment is so vast that the ideal is not functional morally.

2

That this same argument which is so telling against universal benevolence can be used against the effectiveness of the altruistic motive in the nation, the unit with which his social, political, and economic observations are usually concerned, Johnson would be the last to deny. We have already seen that most men are necessarily limited to the sort of indirect beneficence which results from laboring at one's task. This is why there is so little systematic discussion of political and social theory in his works to help the student of his ideas regarding man's broader moral relations. Once Johnson passed from the phase in which he wrote *Marmor Norfolciense* and his other radical pamphlets, once he gave up trying to reform from the top down, his chief concern came to be, as he phrases it in *Idler* No. 70, "to direct the practice of common life," to instruct the individual. He is not interested in theory or, primarily, in disseminating truth, but in bringing about morally correct action. "He that instructs the farmer to plough and sow,

[38] *Works*, II, 469 (*Rambler* No. 99).

may convey his notions without the words which he would find necessary in explaining to philosophers the process of vegetation." Theory is not immediately relevant, and, as we noted earlier, much of Johnson's moral discourse consists of applied psychology and of prudential maxims.

We have a right to expect from such a moralist a succinct statement of what the ordinary man must do, beyond doing the best he can at the task allotted to him. Johnson does not disappoint these expectations. He summed up our duty many times, and a consideration of what he said on these occasions, a return to the practical level, is a fitting conclusion to a chapter largely concerned with his underlying assumptions.

Practical virtue has a number of characteristics. It is seldom the product of motives pure and unmixed. When Mrs. Montagu was accused of ostentatious benevolence, Johnson remarked,

I have seen no beings who do as much good from benevolence, as she does, from whatever motive. . . . No, Sir; to act from pure benevolence is not possible for finite beings. Human benevolence is mingled with vanity, interest, or some other motive.[39]

Practical virtue does not wait for the special occasion.

To do the best can seldom be the lot of man: it is sufficient if, when opportunities are presented, he is ready to do good. How little virtue could be practised, if beneficence were to wait always for the most proper objects, and noblest occasions; occasions that may never happen, and objects that may never be found.[40]

Instead it must often plod on unceasingly as in Levet's case:

> His virtues walk'd their narrow round,
> Nor made a pause, nor left a void;
> And sure th' Eternal Master found
> The single talent well employ'd.[41]

Furthermore, repeated small achievements are superior to the

[39] *Life,* III, 48.
[40] *Works,* VI, 148 (Introduction to *The Proceedings of the Committee* [1760]).
[41] "On the Death of Dr. Robert Levet," lines 25–28 (*Poems,* p. 201).

great design because design is too often a substitute for action. Perhaps the best summary of practical virtue is to be found in *Rasselas,* p. 125. Properly, the search for a way to happiness can have no conclusion; but, however difficult the passage, the way to virtue is clear.

Let us cease to consider what, perhaps, may never happen, and what, when it shall happen, will laugh at human speculation. We will not endeavour to modify the motions of the elements, or to fix the destiny of kingdoms. It is our business to consider what beings like us may perform; each labouring for his own happiness, by promoting within his circle, however narrow, the happiness of others.

For this little sermon Johnson's own career of benevolence is the best exemplum. It would be impossible to enumerate all the tender little anecdotes which have survived, anecdotes like that one which so endeared him to the sister of Sir Joshua Reynolds: "as he return'd to his lodging about one or two o'clock in the morning, he often saw poor children asleep on thresholds and stalls, and . . . he used to put pennies into their hands to buy them a breakfast." [42] And it would be equally futile to attempt to list all those who, like the lunatic, Elizabeth Herne, were more substantially dependent upon his bounty. Most important, such instances as these do not accurately illustrate the real texture of Johnson's beneficent activities, for anyone's heart would feel warmer after slipping coppers into the fingers of such urchins, and if Elizabeth Herne was only a first cousin once removed, she had the merit of being housed at a convenient distance in Bethnal Green. The real measure of Johnson's charity was his household, which was all-too-present, and seldom heart warming.

We do not know much about some of the members of Johnson's household; however, one thing is certain—together they made up an unpleasant company. Even their exact number at any given time would be difficult to determine, because there were many transients, such as the diseased prostitute whom Johnson took in

[42] *Misc.,* II, 251.

and rehabilitated.[43] It is doubtful, though, that these temporary boarders did anything to dilute the unpleasant atmosphere created by the permanent guests. Hawkins says that "even those intruders who had taken shelter under his roof, and who, in his absence from home, brought thither their children, found cause to murmur." Certainly blind Anna Williams justified her presence, but the mutually rewarding nature of her relationship with Johnson tends to obscure the fact that she was utterly incompatible with the rest of the inmates, and often peevish and dictatorial toward him. The negro servant and protégé, Francis Barber, was an ingrate, and, concerning Levet, whatever his essential nobility, it was Johnson's dictum that "his external appearance and behaviour were such, that he disgusted the rich, and terrified the poor." [44]

Although they disagree on many particulars, all of Johnson's friends who wrote important accounts of him are in agreement regarding his household. To show "how uncomfortable his home was made by the perpetual jarring of those whom he charitably accommodated under his roof," Boswell quotes one of Johnson's own letters, "Williams hates everybody; Levett hates Desmoulins, and does not love Williams; Desmoulins hates them both; Poll loves none of them." One of Mrs. Thrale's several accounts of his "wretched household," is typical of the disgust with which she regarded it. She describes Bolt Court in 1782 as a place where "Blind Mrs. Williams, Dropsical Mrs. Desmoulins, Black Francis & his White Wife's Bastard with a wretched Mrs. White, and a Thing that he called Poll; shared his Bounty, & increased his Dirt." [45] Hawkins's bitterly eloquent descriptions are too lengthy to quote, but they leave no doubt as to why, as Johnson admitted, he often turned homeward with hesitant step.

Hawkins, more than the other biographers, seems fascinated by the problem of Johnson's motives in assuming such a burden.

---

[43] The best account is that published by Kearsley and reprinted in *Misc.*, II, 168–169.

[44] *Life of Samuel Johnson*, pp. 408–409, 400.

[45] *Thraliana*, I, 531–532.

Perhaps this preoccupation merely reflects a lack of sympathy with his subject—Sir John is one of those persons, becoming increasingly rare in the 1780's, who seems completely untouched by the altruistic ferment of the age—but Hawkins's wonder does have as its object a very real paradox, for Johnson outdoes many conscientious philanthropists. As we have seen, his contribution toward the founding of Magdalen Hospital was small, he merely gave space in the *Rambler* to a letter pointing out the need for such an institution. On the other hand, one wonders how many of the sincere, dedicated men who were active in establishing the hospital ever carried on the work in their own homes—sheltered a diseased prostitute under their roof until she was well, then set her up in a respectable trade in the country.[46]

Johnson not only denied himself some of the pleasure which

[46] This basic difference is important to a proper assessment of Greene's suggestion that Johnson's humanitarian impulses are Evangelical in origin (*Politics*, pp. 52–54). Even if we grant that the term *Evangelical* is meaningful when applied to the period during which Johnson's humanitarianism was most evident in his writings, the 1750's, there is an element of anachronism in Greene's suggestion, for the Evangelicals were comparative latecomers to the humanitarian movement. It has long been recognized that the doctrinal basis for eighteenth-century altruism was established by a group who were of an entirely different temper from the Evangelicals, the Latitudinarians of the Restoration period. And many of Johnson's most philanthropic contemporaries could not conceivably be regarded as pre-Evangelicals. This is true of Captain Coram, who was responsible for the Foundling Hospital, and also for the early workers in the anti-slavery movement, which was largely Quaker in impulse. Wilberforce, whom Greene cites as a parallel, was not born until 1759, and the seventh Earl of Shaftesbury, not until almost a quarter of a century after Johnson's death. Hannah More, who was thirty-six years younger, might be regarded as a contemporary, and Johnson was quite fond of her—but as a bluestocking, not as an Evangelical reformer. Her real dedication to humanitarian causes came after his death. The one great reformer whose activities were exactly contemporaneous with Johnson's and whose religious practices strongly resemble those of the Evangelicals is Jonas Hanway, and no Johnsonian need have the differences between these two temperaments pointed out to him. Even so, the spirit of Johnson's altruism is closer to Hanway's than it is to that of the true Evangelicals, such as Hannah More and William Wilberforce. These last were praiseworthy and remarkable people, and they are representative of a species which seems essential to our social processes, yet their writings reveal them to have been inspired by a zeal for reform as righteous and doctrinaire as it was idealistic. They tend to look upon much of humanity abstractly and sometimes to fear it. All these qualities are completely foreign to Johnson's humanitarianism and clearly distinguish it from that typical of the eighteenth-century Evangelical.

his modest income could afford him, in order that he might aid these unfortunate, often botched, frequently ungrateful, and usually unattractive, if not actually repellent, people; he also gave up his privacy and his tranquillity. According to his own testimony, especially in the letters to Mrs. Thrale, Johnson in his role of benefactor assumed not only a burden but a hair shirt, too.

It was this aspect of Johnson's charitable activities which puzzled Hawkins. How could a man who was so wise in his moral writings and, to many, so terrifying in company, be at once so imprudent and indulgent at home? [47] Johnson's own explanation of why he chose to aid such people as Poll Carmichael and Mrs. Desmoulins was simply that if he did not, no one would. Sir John's explanation is characteristic; after describing the inmates, he goes on to say with typical prolixity that these

facts and observations are meant to shew some of the most conspicuous features and foibles in Johnson's character, and go to prove, not only that his ferocity was not so terrific, as that anyone endued with temper, and disposed to moderation and forbearance, might not only withstand, but overcome it, but that he had a natural imbecility about him, arising from humanity and pity to the sufferings of his fellow-creatures, that was prejudicial to his interests; and also, that he neither sought nor expected praise for those acts of beneficence which he was daily performing, nor looked for any retribution from those who were nourished by his bounty.[48]

Another biographer, Thomas Tyers, put it more gracefully: "His charities were many; only not so extensive as his pity, for that was universal." [49] Johnson himself always insisted that firm precepts and a strong sense of duty are necessary to make pity effective, and, certainly, force of will must have acted in league with compassion in Johnson's charitable activity, for he seems intentionally to renounce or negate by his choice of beneficiaries much of the pleasure to be derived from giving. Hawkins is close

[47] See especially his *Life of Samuel Johnson,* pp. 405–413.
[48] *Life of Samuel Johnson,* p. 413. See also p. 410.
[49] *Misc.,* II, 378.

to a solution when speaking in another connection he cites a sentiment from Thomas à Kempis which Johnson greatly applauded.

> It is no great matter to live lovingly with good-natured, with humble and meek persons; but he who can do so with the froward, with the wilful, and the ignorant, with the peevish and perverse, he only hath true charity.[50]

Hawkins did not err when he charged Johnson with being imprudent; the moralist's inability to live by his own precepts has been remarked by many succeeding critics. Nor can it be denied that much of the energy which characterizes his moral essays derives from the fact that the problems had an immediate relevance for him, that he was daily wrestling with them and was often vanquished. It is also plausible to maintain, as some have, that Johnson considered by his own standards was a failure morally. He was often proud, contentious, and domineering; he was given to all sorts of vain fears, wishes, and imaginings; he was slothful and gluttonous.

But morals are not just a matter of prudence, nor do they stop with the individual's relationship to himself. Johnson is typical of his century in that he makes conduct toward others the final test of morality. His answer to the question, "What is the moral life?" is based on utilitarian and altruistic principles which, as we have seen, permeate his thinking on political, economic, and social problems. For the individual the answer as it applies to everyday life is simple, clear, and perhaps, all the more challenging, because it embodies Johnson's intense awareness of man's limitations: he must work, making the best of whatever abilities have been allotted him, and he must promote "within his circle, however narrow, the happiness of others."

This is the precept by which Johnson's conduct must be tried and his personal merit vindicated. The hours and years he wasted

---

[50] *Life of Samuel Johnson,* p. 543. He is actually citing an adaptation by Jeremy Taylor from *Polemical and Moral Discourses* (1657), p. 25.

do not diminish the magnitude of his accomplishment as a moralist, critic, and lexicographer. He made fruitful use of remarkable abilities which were counterpoised by extraordinary handicaps. Finally, compassion alone is not enough to account for his choice of recipients for his charity, and especially for his loyalty to that choice. He must also have patience, humility, and a strong sense of duty, who will remain faithful to the peevish and perverse, the ungrateful and the ignorant.

❦ VI ❧

The Bases of Morality

Johnson's practical ethic is so unsystematic that only a fool would expect to find an elaborate, regular theory underlying it. Yet it is justifiable to inquire into what Johnson means by *good* when he tells us, for instance, that self-knowledge is good, or by *duty,* when he declares that beneficence is our duty. Johnson's failure to arrange his moral notions into complex patterns does not rule out the possibility that he may have done some thinking on the fundamental problems of ethics in an orderly or, at least, consistent manner.

It may well be that the immediate source of his practical statements is some muddied and turbulent fountain of anxieties and other drives—for some time now it has been the fashion to depict Johnson as the most eminently irrational product of an age which is still celebrated, rightly or wrongly, as an era of calm and practical good sense. Even if this is the case, we must investigate these impulses—while avoiding the temptation to perform any new psychological analyses—because whatever proportions of reason, emotion, and instinct are responsible for his moral fervor, it is obvious that Johnson's practical moralizing springs directly from convictions so powerful that no discussion of him as a moralist can be complete unless they are considered.

Only one of Johnson's essays is of much help in devising an orderly approach to his unsystematic moral convictions, the review of Soame Jenyns's *Free Enquiry into the Nature and Origin of Evil*. Johnson's comments on Jenyns's attempt to classify ethical theories are particularly useful to us, and they carry all the more weight because he never bestows praise on Jenyns freely. Johnson begins by saying that

the first pages of the fourth letter are such, as incline me both to hope and wish that I shall find nothing to blame in the succeeding part. He offers a criterion of action, on account of virtue and vice, for which I have often contended, and which must be embraced by all who are willing to know, why they act, or why they forbear to give any reason of their conduct to themselves or others.

And then he reprints these pages in full. The heart of Jenyns's argument is contained in this passage:

They who extol the truth, beauty, and harmony of virtue, exclusive of its consequences, deal but in pompous nonsense; and they, who would persuade us, that good and evil are things indifferent, depending wholly on the will of God, do but confound the nature of things, as well as all our notions of God himself, by representing him capable of willing contradictions. . . . It is the consequences, therefore, of all human actions that must stamp their value. So far as the general practice of any action tends to produce good, and introduce happiness into the world, so far may we pronounce it virtuous; so much evil as it occasions, such is the degree of vice it contains.[1]

In other words, an action is morally commendable not because it proceeds from a beautifully virtuous character, or because it is

[1] *Works*, VI, 66–68.

produced by obedience to some edict, but on account of its results. Morality can be regarded as principally a matter of virtue, of duty, or of consequences; and the last of these is the true criterion. To this Johnson responds eloquently, "Si sic omnia dixisset!" and proceeds to add a lengthy proviso on the dangers of seeking to penetrate remote consequences, which qualifies Jenyns's thesis but slightly.

Of course, it would be putting too much stress on a single statement to accept as definitive Johnson's rejections of the two approaches to morality, and then proceed to analyze the third, which he accepts—consequences as criterion. But perhaps the three criteria can be used to provide a framework, as points of reference, in analyzing the convictions which underlie Johnson's practical moralizing.

An interesting aspect of this classification which Johnson endorses so enthusiastically is its resemblance to that devised by the late Professor John Laird of Aberdeen, one of the most stimulating writers on British empiricism, in his *Enquiry into Moral Notions* (1935). Laird felt that all moral notions can ultimately be referred to one or another of three terms—virtue, duty, or benefit—and that these terms are irreducible. According to Laird, the same ultimate criteria underlie systematic ethical philosophies which Jenyns and Johnson see as governing more popular and less abstruse moral thought.

David Hume, for example, often propounds an ethic of virtue, despite his utilitarian bent.

'Tis evident, that when we praise any actions, we regard only the motives that produced them, and consider the actions as signs or indications of certain principles in the mind and temper. The external performance has no merit. We must look within to find the moral quality.

But these "principles" are elements of character not principles of duty, for *"no action can be virtuous, or morally good, unless there be in human nature some motive to produce it, distinct from the sense of its morality."* [2]

In what is essentially a reply to Hume, Immanuel Kant comes as close as anyone ever has to a pure ethic of duty. Notice how he depreciates the role of temperament or character in his interpretation of the text "Thou shalt love thy neighbor as thyself":

Love, as an affection, cannot be commanded, but beneficence for duty's sake may; even though we are not impelled to it by any inclination—nay, are even repelled by a natural and unconquerable aversion. This is *practical* love, and not *pathological*—a love which is seated in the will, and not in the propensions of sense—in principles of action and not tender sympathy; and it is this love alone which can be commanded.[3]

He goes on to dismiss the ethic of benefit just as peremptorily as he did that of virtue, when he states "that the purposes which we may have in view in our action or their effects regarded as ends and springs of the will, cannot give to actions any unconditional or moral worth."

Opposed to both of these fundamental attitudes is the moralist who stresses benefit, a figure who has become familiar enough since Johnson's day that no example need be cited. He concerns himself with actions and results, and he insists that it is the end achieved which governs the morality of an action, not the character from which it proceeds or the sense of duty behind it.

Of course, no one of these three criteria need predominate; a moralist may stress first one and then another, even though most tend to emphasize just one. To return to the practical level, consider the most popular devotional work of eighteenth-century England, William Law's *A Serious Call to a Devout and Holy Life*. In an apparent attempt to consider all phases of religious morality, Law organized the book so that virtue, duty, and benefit

---

[2] *A Treatise of Human Nature*, ed. L. A. Selby-Bigge (Oxford, 1888), pp. 477, 479. These examples are cited by Laird.

[3] *Fundamental Principles of the Metaphysics of Morals*, trans. Thomas K. Abbott (Chicago, 1949), p. 17.

are each taken up separately. The first four chapters deal with the "virtues" and "tempers" of Christians, and in them Law insists that men must possess "the *intention* to please God in all their actions." In the fifth chapter the text changes abruptly from "the intention to please God," to the absolute necessity for obedience to divine will: "Our blessed Saviour has plainly turn'd our thoughts this way, by making this petition a constant part of all our prayers, *Thy will be done on earth, as it is in heaven.*" Throughout the following chapters the terms of a duty ethic constantly recur—"law," "rule," "command," "duty," "obligation." We cannot expect Law to give benefit equal status with Christian virtue and obedience to duty, but the last three chapters before he turns from morality to formal devotion are given over to "shewing how great devotion fills our lives with the greatest peace and happiness that can be enjoy'd in this life" and that lack of devotion will produce misery and disquiet.

Such a balanced point of view is uncommon among popular moralists of Johnson's time, especially is it rare in purely secular writers. That increasing emphasis on the emotions which we have already discussed, results in what is predominantly an ethic of virtue. Strictly speaking, virtue is a quality which inheres in the individual moral agent, and it is of this sort of criterion which Johnson's contemporaries are stressing at the expense of all other considerations when they center their attentions on benevolent emotions, when they assume that if individuals are goodhearted, worthy actions and beneficial results will follow automatically.

In Chapter II, I made the obvious suggestion that the growing emphasis on emotion in morals is related to the change in the concept of the rational faculty and that Johnson is antagonistic toward sentimental morality because he is devoted to the ideals of freedom and responsibility which were bound up with the traditional humanistic notion that the reason is supreme in ethics. Another factor in the rise of sentimental morality is the growing optimism regarding human nature. To base morality on good affections one must feel sure that either man's emotions are naturally good, or that good ones can be easily planted or nurtured in the human breast. Here, too, is an aspect of sentimental morality bound to arouse opposition in the pessimistic Johnson.

To choose an extreme example of this optimism, it is easy to imagine how Johnson must have reacted on that day when he was trapped in a stagecoach with nothing to read but Laurence Sterne's *Sermons,* if he got as far as the seventh one, where Yorick tells his readers that if they observe a typical young man, as yet untouched by the disillusioning world, they

> will find that one of the first and leading propensities of his nature is that, which discovers itself in the desire of society, and the spontaneous love towards those of his kind. . . . Agreeably to this, observe how warmly, how heartily he enters into friendships,—how disinterested, and unsuspicious in the choice of them,—how generous and open in his professions!—how sincere and honest in making them good!—When his friend is in distress,—what lengths he will go,—what hazards he will bring upon himself,—what embarrassment upon his affairs to extricate and serve him! [4]

In other words, the only thing wrong with human nature and emotions is that the world corrupts them.

No one today is likely to think of Sterne as a moralist, even when he speaks from the pulpit, but on such optimistic estimates of humanity as his was based the cult of feeling—what might be termed a pseudo-ethic of virtue—which sanctioned the pleasurable pastime of emoting for emotion's sake, on the pretext that emotion is all that matters in morality and that good emotions are so efficacious that actions and their results need not be regarded at all.

Oliver Goldsmith, to choose another example, professes to hate feelers as intensely as Johnson does, yet in his attack on sentimentalism he is trying to purify the springs of behavior, to cultivate those seeds of benevolence which according to his own more favorable estimate are planted in the human character. The benevolent affections are to be exercised disinterestedly for good

---

[4] Laurence Sterne, *The Sermons of Mr. Yorick* (New York, 1904), I, 117–118.

ends, not for the sake of pleasure or applause. Therefore, Goldsmith's paragon of virtue, the Man in Black who appears in "The Citizen of the World," is the antithesis of a feeler. He affects misanthropy in order to conceal "virtues which others take such pains to display," while within, he positively seethes with benevolent emotions, and at the sight of distress "his heart is dilated with the most unbounded love," "his cheek glows with compassion," his looks soften with pity. According to Goldsmith, the sentimentalist is wrong not because he exaggerates the importance of benevolent emotions but because he perverts them.

Even Henry Fielding, who is opposite to Sterne in so many respects, shares with him the contemporary disposition to make morals principally a matter of character and emotion.[5] With Goldsmith, he insists that the only reliable test of good nature is good works. Unlike him, and unlike Sterne, Fielding is not sanguine in his attitude toward the raw stuff of human nature. Man is often dominated by his passions, sometimes, Fielding suggests, by a ruling passion, and, as Booth discovers, the prospect of Divine rewards and punishment is necessary to make men behave. Yet because he conceives of goodness in terms of good nature, Fielding's is no less an ethic of virtue than the sentimentalists', and, as with them, it is optimism which distinguishes him from Johnson, his faith that once benevolent emotions are established in an individual's breast, they become a strong-flowing and steady spring of good actions.

Johnson's pessimism prevents him from accepting even that mild form of sentimental morality preached by Henry Fielding. Johnson doubts the efficacy of good intentions, he suspects human motives, and he feels that "the depravity of mankind is so easily discoverable, that nothing but the desert or the cell can exclude it from notice." [6] As might be expected, many people were shocked by these sentiments. Their reactions range all the way from the

---

[5] A concise and perceptive summary of Fielding's moral notions is given by George Sherburn in his "Fielding's Social Outlook," *PQ*, XXXV (1956), 1–23.

[6] *Works*, III, 322 (*Rambler* No. 175).

relatively mild protests of Mrs. Chapone and of Lady MacLeod, who, when she asked if no man were naturally good, got the reply, "No madam, no more than a wolf," to William Mudford's vituperative comments on the *Rambler:*

What a depraved picture of human nature is this! In what a world of infamy and guilt do we exist! Where shall we seek for friendship where all are false; where shall we repose our griefs where none are virtuous? Alas! How may the most exalted intellect be corrupted by a pernicious indulgence of rancorous prejudices? [7]

It is true that Johnson became somewhat more optimistic as he grew older, but this is chiefly because he tempered his expectations and became more tolerant of human failings.

Perhaps it is this pessimism which provokes the occasional critic to call Johnson a Calvinist. The accusation is unfair, as we saw in Chapter II, yet excusable, because often Johnson seems to feel that man has no more freedom than the bare minimum necessary to make moral struggle worthwhile. Beneficence, the cardinal virtue, is acquired, not innate, for "naturally a child seizes directly what it sees, and thinks of pleasing itself only. By degrees, it is taught to please others, and to prefer others; and that this will ultimately produce the greatest happiness." [8] Nor is complacence ever in order once the lessons of morality have been learned: "to contend with the predominance of successive passions, to be endangered first by one affection, and then by another, is the condition upon which we are to pass our time." [9]

If Laird is correct in his assumption that no moralist can completely disregard any one of the three criteria—virtue, duty, or benefit—we should expect Johnson to concern himself with virtue part of the time, and, of course, this is the case. He is even willing to grant that "we have a certain degree of feeling to prompt us to do good," but adds, "more than that, Providence does not in-

[7] *A Critical Enquiry into the Moral Writings of Dr. Samuel Johnson* (1802), p. 24.

[8] *Life,* V, 211 (*Journal of a Tour to the Hebrides*).

[9] *Works,* III, 219 (*Rambler* No. 151).

tend." [10] And, like all practical moralists, Johnson is very much concerned with developing virtuous traits of character among his readers. In fact, he believes that happiness is to a large extent dependent upon the formation of proper habits of mind. But virtue or good character is to Johnson's way of thinking instrumental and never complete in itself. Although character is quite important practically, the moral quality of an action does not ultimately depend on the goodness or badness, the virtue or vice, of the one who performs it.

Illustrative of Johnson's feelings about the relationship of the springs of a given action to its morality are his remarks on motive and intent. Some of these comments are very typical of the time. For instance, on the day when Boswell first visited him in his chambers, Johnson declared that

the morality of an action depends on the motive from which we act. If I fling half a crown to a beggar with intention to break his head, and he picks it up and buys victuals with it, the physical effect is good; but with respect to me, the action is very wrong. [11]

And many years later he remarked in a similar vein that "if a profuse man, who does not value his money, and gives a large sum to a whore, gives half as much, or an equally large sum to relieve a friend, it cannot be esteemed as virtue." [12]

Sometimes Johnson's statements reflect his age's insistence that disinterested benevolence is the only source of true charity. In his most effective sermon on charity, the fourth, he warns his listeners that Divine favor cannot be won by that sort of beneficence which is prompted by a desire for applause or for some other personal gratification. Nor can beneficence be wholly a matter of doing one's duty either. It is commanded that we be just to our fellow-beings, but the rule

is not equally determinate and absolute, with respect to offices of

---

[10] *Life*, II, 94. See also *Works*, IX, 322 (Sermon IV).
[11] *Life*, I, 397–398.
[12] *Life*, III, 195.

kindness, and acts of liberality, because liberality and kindness, absolutely determined, would lose their nature; for how could we be called tender, or charitable, for giving that which we are absolutely forbidden to withhold? [13]

Good intentions may be necessary if the doer of a beneficial action is to gain any merit by it, but they do not excuse an act which turns out to be harmful. In this conviction Johnson runs counter to the spirit of eighteenth-century popular morality, which he accurately characterizes when he notes that "there is no topick more the favourite of the present age, than the innocence of errour accompanied with sincerity." [14]

In this remark one can discern Johnson's dogged and practical empiricism, which is as much a barrier to his acceptance of any ethic based principally on character or virtue, as his pessimism regarding human nature. It is comparatively easy to determine whether an action conforms to some principle of duty or whether the proximate results are good, but frequently it is very difficult to ascertain the true motive behind it. Even the actor may not know what his motive is, and if he does, he may not be willing to admit it to himself or to others. If too much stress is put upon virtuous motives, the morality of an action cannot be verified in a quarter where objective comparison is possible; instead it must be determined in the confused shadowland of impulse, appetite, and emotion. It was not just prejudice which caused Johnson to react so violently when Boswell remarked, with what may have been mock innocence, that he believed Rousseau meant well:

Sir, that will not do. We cannot prove any man's intention to be bad. You may shoot a man through the head, and say you intended to miss him; but the Judge will order you to be hanged. An alledged want of intention, when evil is committed, will not be allowed in a court of justice.[15]

Johnson concedes that good motives are a neecssary condition if any action is to confer merit on the one who performs it, but he

[13] *Works,* II, 381–382 (*Rambler* No. 81).
[14] *Works,* IX, 354 (Sermon VII).
[15] *Life,* II, 12.

insists that they can never in themselves be a sufficient condition for terming any action good.

The moral life is a life of constant activity. It is this belief that most decisively sets Johnson apart from those moralists who emphasize character and virtue. We have already seen many examples of his insistence that morality is not primarily a matter of being something, or even of becoming something, but of doing. Witness, his disdain for escapists and recluses. The cloisterer may be of spotless virtue; he may be wise and know all things, but a truly good man he cannot be, because a good man strives. "It cannot be allowed, that flight is victory; or that he fills his place in creation laudably, who does no ill, *only* because he does *nothing*." [16] Or, as Thomas Nettleton, a contemporary moralist, pungently phrased it, "the religious recluse hopes to merit heaven by being good for nothing on earth."

Activity is so tightly and uniformly woven into the texture of Johnson's moral notions that by examining the motives behind his insistence on it and selecting those which he seems to regard as most urgent, it should be possible to discover his basic moral convictions. Or, to put it in terms of the criteria which he himself thought of as characterizing the different approaches to morals, it should be possible to find out whether Johnson thinks men should act because it is their duty to do so, or, whether as he claims in his review of Jenyns's *Enquiry,* for the sake of the resulting benefits. And if consequences are the criterion, we should be able to determine the nature of these ultimate benefits or ends.

Sometimes the activity which Johnson recommends in his moral essays is merely instrumental or prudential. It consists of what he calls in the twelfth Sermon "actions of necessity," which involve no moral choice. On one level, his poem "The Ant" deals with this motive to action:

> How long shall sloth usurp thy useless hours,
> Dissolve thy vigour, and enchain thy powers?
> While artful shades thy downy couch enclose,

[16] *Works,* IX, 313 (Sermon III).

> And soft solicitation courts repose,
> Amidst the drousy charms of dull delight,
> Year chases year, with unremitted flight,
> Till want, now following fraudulent and slow,
> Shall spring to seize thee like an ambush'd foe.[17]

More often there are ethical issues involved. In the first place, he feels so strongly that idleness is the mother of vice, that on occasion he is willing to recommend almost any sort of activity, no matter how frivolous, in preference to it. In defense of a company of virtuosos, he says that "whatever busies the mind without corrupting it, has at least this use, that it rescues the day from idleness, and he that is never idle will not often be vicious." [18] And even mild dissipation is preferable to some of the passions which idleness breeds:

As Idleness is apt to give opportunities for the Cultivation of that Sensibility which is always blunted by Employment, so says he it nurses all evil and prurient Passions; and it is upon this Principle that Mr. Johnson recommends Dissipation to those who are but poorly supplied with intellectual Entertainment.[19]

Behind these traditional comments is Johnson's belief that "the old peripatetick principle, that *Nature abhors a vacuum,* may be properly applied to the intellect, which will embrace anything, however absurd or criminal, rather than be wholly without an object." [20] According to Mrs. Thrale he constantly referred to this notion:

The vacuity of Life had at some early Period in his Life perhaps so struck upon the Mind of Mr. Johnson, that it became by repeated Impression his favourite hypothesis. . . . all was done to fill up the Time upon his Principle. one Man for example was profligate, followed the Girls or the Gaming Table,—why Life *must* be filled up Madam, & the Man was capable of nothing less Sensual.[21]

---

[17] *Poems,* 151–152.
[18] *Works,* III, 333 (*Rambler* No. 178).
[19] *Thraliana,* I, 180.
[20] *Works,* II, 402.
[21] *Thraliana,* I, 179. See also I, 254.

The thought of this boredom, this vacuity of life which always must be filled up, often was in itself more appalling to Johnson than some of the vices bred by it. Here we may seem to wander for a moment from the moral doctrines to approach closer to the man himself, but there is no need to apologize, because naturally the distinction between the two will grow more tenuous as we deal more with basic convictions. Of course, there is some danger in assuming, as scholars do occasionally, that Johnson's moral writings are actually essays in self-criticism, that he is usually prescribing for his own maladies. Although Johnson knows the human heart and mind so well only because he sees himself with such disquieting clarity, it seems prudent to assume that as a moralist he has objective control of both his personae and his topics, and that the choice of topics is dictated by his notion of what it is in his readers which most needs correction.

Yet, when his biographers repeatedly point out a specific weakness in his character it is safe to assume that he has his own predicament in mind when he prescribes for the weakness. The letter of Dick Linger in *Idler* No. 21 is certainly such an instance; here Johnson describes the balance of opposing forces which results in the dreary equilibrium of boredom and apathy:

Those only will sympathize with my complaint, whose imagination is active, and resolution weak, whose desires are ardent, and whose choice is delicate; who cannot satisfy themselves with standing still, and yet cannot find a motive to direct their course.

This dead calm is so unbearable that men will risk their lives to break free from it. Johnson feels that those soldiers who desire war most "are neither prompted by malevolence nor patriotism; they neither pant for laurels, nor delight in blood; but long to be delivered from the tyranny of idleness, and restored to the dignity of active beings." [22] And it is hard to disagree with him.

Johnson's insomnia served to intensify the particular dilemma which his own indolence bred. There are perhaps less than twenty

[22] *Works,* IV, 210, 211.

references to his sleeplessness available to us, but those comments which have survived disclose that the intensity of his malady was all out of proportion to the number of allusions to it. We know, for instance, that next to the anniversary of his wife's death, March 28th, the date to which Johnson's memory most often turned during his last decade was August 30, 1773, when he had enjoyed such a remarkable sleep at Fort Augustus in the Highlands. Six years before this memorable occasion, on an evening when he feels he will be able to rest, he prays hopefully in his *Prayers and Meditations* that "perhaps this may be such a sudden relief as I once had by a good night's rest in Fetter Lane." This means that he clearly recalls a night of sleep which he enjoyed, at the very least, eighteen years before.

Johnson's insomnia may have been more severe than that experienced by most men, but his symptoms are familiar enough. He is perturbed at night and irresolute and listless by day, so that he can work only "by sudden snatches." An especially active imagination such as Johnson's adds to the tortures of insomnia, for in bed the wits remain keen, and vivid images flit through the mind at an astonishing speed. Connections never before perceived become as clear as if they had always been known. In a sense, the insomniac is most creative when he suffers most. Yet the visions can be terrible, and, if they are not, the victim becomes depressed anyhow when he tries to make use of them, because the remarkable fabrics dissolve away as rapidly as they appeared, leaving their creator enervated and apathetic after the briefest spurt of real activity.

Bate is certainly correct in relating Johnson's insomnia to his fear of death, but it is one of those paradoxes so typical of human nature that on a purely conscious level, Johnson actually fears not going to sleep, the most corrosive of all the anxieties which afflict the insomniac.[23] In 1772 Johnson writes to John Taylor that he has lost command of his own attention,

---

[23] *The Achievement of Samuel Johnson* (New York, 1955), p. 160.

Of this power which is of the highest importance to the tranquillity of life, I have for some time past been so much exhausted, that I do not go into a company towards night in which I forsee anything disagreeable, nor enquire after any thing to which I am not indifferent, lest something, which I know to be nothing, should fasten upon my imagination, and hinder me from sleep.[24]

Not just some special anxiety, but almost any concern can dilate to become the thief of his repose. And so Johnson was ensnared by a malady insidiously circular in its workings: Anxiety or the physical discomfort he suffered for most of his life keeps him awake. When day comes he is indolent because of fatigue and accomplishes nothing, and this in turn arouses guilt and the fear that the experience will be repeated. If, by chance, he is able to fall asleep toward morning and "is tempted to repair the deficiencies of the night," the time lost while he dawdles in bed also breeds guilty anxieties, which do their work the next night. Thus, the disease feeds upon itself, making Johnson increasingly subject to a vacuity and indolence from which he is progressively less and less capable of escaping.

As W. B. C. Watkins aptly put it, "the Castle of Indolence is merely a way-station to the Cave of Despair." There are innumerable conjectures as to the causes and nature of Johnson's melancholy;[25] however, for our purposes his own account in "The Vision of Theodore, Hermit of Teneriffe" (1748) is sufficient to show why he considered action the best therapy:

There were others . . . who retreated from the heat and tumult of the way, not to the bowers of Intemperance, but to the maze of Indolence. . . . They wandered on from one double of the labyrinth to another with the chains of Habit hanging secretly upon them, till, as they advanced, the flowers grew paler, and the scents fainter; they proceeded in their dreary march without pleasure in their progress, yet without power to return; and had this aggravation above all others, that they were criminal but not delighted. The drunkard . . . laughed

[24] *Letters*, I, 281.
[25] The most satisfying discussion is still that of W. B. C. Watkins in his *Perilous Balance* (Princeton, 1939).

over his wine; the ambitious man triumphed in the miscarriage of his rival; but the captives of Indolence had neither superiority nor merriment. Discontent lowered in their looks, and sadness hovered round their shades; yet they crawled on reluctant and gloomy, till they arrived at the depth of the recess, varied only with poppies and nightshade, where the dominion of Indolence terminates, and the hopeless wanderer is delivered up to Melancholy; the chains of Habit are rivetted for ever; and Melancholy, having tortured her prisoner for a time, consigns him at last to the cruelty of Despair.[26]

There may be some question regarding what it was that Johnson found at the end of the dreary march, but there is none concerning the intensity with which he dreaded what was waiting there or what measures he proposed for avoiding it.

Fortunately, few of us are so severely afflicted with melancholy as Johnson was, and his prescription for driving off the black dog will be but intermittently useful to most men. And even in Johnson's case, the usefulness of activity as a preventive for melancholy does not fully explain why he recommended it so strongly. Prudence may dictate acting, idleness may breed vice, despair may be wrong and certainly it is painful, but none of these circumstances accounts for the intensity of the guilty anguish which Johnson felt whenever he reflected upon his past indolence.

In *The Achievement of Samuel Johnson*, W. J. Bate demonstrates that Johnson assigns to activity still another therapeutic function more profound in its implications and universally relevant. It is a means to a generally healthful mind, and to human fulfillment—"the developing and completing of human nature." Bate focuses on the peculiar dilemma which confronts man because of the way imagination and desire interact to produce hope. As Mary Lascelles describes the situation in her essay "Rasselas Reconsidered,"

man, forbidden to despair, is bound for disappointment: he is forever dissatisfied because he must seek the satisfaction proper to his nature

[26] *Works*, IX, 174–175.

elsewhere, but what he is, here, forever hinders this search. Thus he becomes an inveterate gambler with hope.[27]

This is so, Bate says, because "in the very activity or process of wishing, there are inherent liabilities that are able to undercut the wish itself—the liabilities that the 'capacity of the imagination' is always so 'much larger than actual enjoyment,' and that nevertheless it tends to simplify, to fix on a specific object." These objects are unstable, but even if they were not, our ability to enjoy them would be.[28]

This phenomenon involves what I described in Chapter I in rather graceless terms as future psychological hedonism. Johnson repeatedly asserts his conviction that man never is, but is always to be, blessed: "that man is never happy for the present is so true, that all his relief from unhappiness is only forgetting himself for a little while. Life is a progress from want to want, not from enjoyment to enjoyment." [29] However, there is a paradox involved, which is expressed in Thomas Campbell's couplet:

> Thus, with delight, we linger to survey
> The promised joys of life's unmeasured way.

Semantically want cannot be enjoyment, but it is delight or pleasure and, thus, want, not enjoyment provides most of the happiness we are allotted in the present state. Rasselas is being quite logical when he exclaims "I have already enjoyed too much; give me something to desire," for, "attainment is followed by neglect, and possession by disgust," but hope, the product of desire and imagination, is ever green.

Future psychological hedonism is not what the eighteenth century would consider a moral principle; it merely describes the working of the mind. Therefore, controlling this particular process is more a matter of prudence than morality. Most of our

[27] *Essays and Studies*, New Series, IV (1951), 45.
[28] *The Achievement of Samuel Johnson*, pp. 81–82.
[29] *Life*, III, 53.

happiness may come from desiring, but so does much of our pain, as we learn from episode after episode in *Rasselas*. Johnson says in one of his letters that "hope is itself a species of happiness, & perhaps the chief happiness which this World affords, but like all other pleasures immoderately enjoyed, the excesses of hope must be expiated by pain, & expectations improperly indulged must end in disappointment." [30]

Nevertheless, Bate feels that Johnson considers this continual activity of desiring to be morally formative under the proper circumstances. If it is turned inward, it will operate destructively and isolate the individual, but when the process is turned outward, and active links of sympathy and understanding with what is outside are formed, the individual will grow and profit. We "project ourselves forward—into our future condition . . . and bend our efforts to secure it," only if we are "able to turn outside our present sensations in another way, and lose the sense of our 'personal identity' in some *other* object," only if we have not isolated ourselves.[31]

Bate's interpretation of Johnson does involve a serious problem. Mere growing outward is not development, because process is not inherently beneficial. Cancer is a process. Presumably the individual will profit through trial and error, but life is too short for most men to lift themselves very high by this means. There must be some shaping end toward which the organism strives, or there must be some implicit pattern or potency which the organism fulfills, such as that of the oak in the acorn. Unless there is a formative element involved, Johnson's concept depends on the end-in-view and necessarily suffers from that same defect which consigned the principal American contribution to ethics, Pragmatism, to the philosophical rag bag.

This question is especially pertinent where Johnson is concerned, because despite his sloth he has more than his share of

---

[30] *Letters,* I, 137.
[31] *The Achievement of Samuel Johnson,* 139–140.

that Dionysian impulse which we all possess, the urge to act, not in order to attain anything, but simply to be doing.

To strive with difficulties, and to conquer them, is the highest human felicity; the next is, to strive, and to deserve to conquer: but he whose life has passed without a contest, and who can boast neither success nor merit, can survey himself only as a useless filler of existence; and if he is content with his own character, must owe his satisfaction to insensibility.[32]

The term *useless* applied to the idler suggests that Johnson has some sort of overriding purpose in mind here; yet what he is celebrating is activity itself, pure striving, not desire and enjoyment of some immediate end, not movement toward some ultimate end, not development or self-realization. This impulse to activity is almost never pure; on the other hand, more frequently than we realize, ends are contrived to satisfy its urgings. The purer it becomes, the more ethical problems it creates—this is our concern with it. Some formidable metaphysical arguments can be erected upon the hypothesis of flux, but for the moralist's creations it affords a slippery and insecure foundation.

Bate answers the question as to what it is which gives form and direction to this growth by pointing to Johnson's deep longing for the stability of truth. This is the shaping end toward which the organism strives. He remarks that human development

involves not the rejection but the use of primary human capacities—an active "concord and harmony," as Plato said, "of definite and particular pleasures and appetites." Furthermore, almost all of these pleasures or appetites have within themselves a *potential* yearning—perhaps too blind to be called desire—to reassure themselves and to work toward reality. As Johnson said, the "heart naturally loves truth"—it wants, at least, the security which truth alone can give.[33]

It is possible to quarrel about some details of this ethic of self-realization. If, for instance, one accepts the proposition that

---

[32] *Works,* IV, 108–109 (*Adventurer* No. 111).
[33] *The Achievement of Samuel Johnson,* p. 140.

Johnson's theory of knowledge is largely derived from Locke, Bate's thesis presents some formidable epistemological difficulties. But it is unquestionably true that Johnson regards the fulfillment of man's potentialities as one of the ultimate ends of morality. No one could witness his repeated insistence that social beings must strive to live up to their capabilities and the lacerating guilt he felt when he thought he was wasting his own powers and not grant this.

I think that the importance of the principle of self-realization in Johnson's moral thinking can be confirmed by considering what he has to say about the nature of happiness. Although happiness may as a will-o-the-wisp delude man into an unending chase through bewildering and often treacherous bogs, Johnson never does deny that it is something real and substantial, a good of the highest order. The fault lies not in the goal but in the the manner men quest after it and, especially, in their ignorance of its true nature.

Practical moralists are often vague when they come to describe the nature of ultimate goods, but Johnson's readers could hardly plead this excuse with respect to happiness, for he speaks explicitly concerning its various qualities, even though he offers no neat and concise definition. Happiness should not, for instance, be confused with mere pleasure. The latter which Johnson defines as immediate "gratification of the mind or senses," is certainly a good, but he so hedges it about with restrictions that it can serve as a very limited end, at best. It is true that we naturally seek pleasure and that it is imprudent or foolish to spurn pleasure when it may be enjoyed without guilt. Johnson became more and more convinced as he grew older that "when pleasure can be had it is fit to catch it: Every hour takes away part of the things that please us, and perhaps part of our disposition to be pleased." [34] On the other hand, many pleasures are directly evil and some it is imprudent to enjoy. Throughout his more sober essays Johnson

[34] *Letters*, II, 198.

admonishes his readers that they often will be called on to make the traditional choice of Hercules, between virtue and pleasure.[35] And frequently he consoles them with the sentiment that in Heaven "pleasure and virtue will be perfectly consistent."

The superiority of happiness derives from a number of characteristics. In the first place, despite the *Dictionary,* Johnson commonly thinks of happiness as rational or mental, as opposed to pleasure, which he conceives of as more sensuous—sometimes wholly sensuous, as when in the course of what is a rather calm argument with Boswell he says "When we talk of pleasure, we mean sensual pleasure. . . . Philosophers tell you, that pleasure is *contrary* to happiness. Gross men prefer animal pleasure."[36] Secondly, unlike pleasures, happiness is usually complex; it "consists in the multiplicity of agreeable consciousness." Because he believes happiness to be complex, Johnson agrees with Locke and contradicts Hume in maintaining that it cannot be the subject of any simple calculus, "Sir, that all who are happy, are equally happy, is not true. A peasant and a philosopher may be equally *satisfied,* but not equally *happy.* . . . A peasant has not capacity for having equal happiness with a philosopher." And these differences in the human capacity for happiness are qualitative as well as quantitative, for "our Maker, who, though he gave us such varieties of temper and such difference of powers, yet designed us all for happiness, undoubtedly intended that we should obtain that happiness by different means."[37]

Johnson's concept of happiness has its dynamic aspects, too. As we have seen, it is not a passive state of placid contentment. "Life affords no higher pleasure than that of surmounting difficulties, passing from one step to another, forming new wishes, and seeing them gratified." Rather than the satisfaction of specific

---

[35] See the frontispiece to the *Preceptor* for a pictorial representation of this very common eighteenth-century theme.

[36] *Life,* III, 246. See also *Rasselas,* p. 15.

[37] *Life,* II, 9; *Works,* IV, 127 (*Adventurer* No. 126). A similar statement is made by Locke in a quotation used by Johnson under *happiness* in the *Dictionary.*

desires, often it is the process itself which gives happiness, the satisfaction of having striven well, whether all our objectives are attained or not. Legitimate self-esteem plays an important role, which is the reason why it is so difficult to remain idle and happy.[38]

Something more than simple activity is involved in this dynamic concept of happiness. For one so pessimistic regarding human motives and human fortunes Johnson upon occasion is remarkably sanguine about the possibility of human progress, collective and individual. He is thinking of moral progress, however. Something can be done about slavery, for instance, because from his point of view the problem is moral, not sociological or economic. Johnson's most judicious statement of this faith in reformation which all moralists must possess is in the last *Adventurer* where he takes stock of what he has accomplished, and comes to the conclusion that "the progress of reformation is gradual and silent, as the evening shadows." And three years later, to Soame Jenyns's doubts that man was created perfect, Johnson replies that "the perfection which man once had, may be so easily conceived, that, without any unusual strain of imagination, we can figure its revival." [39] This perfection is depicted in the sixth Sermon, where Johnson writes of his Utopia, a society in which all are happy because all are virtuous.

Utopia will never come, and any progress toward it must be painfully slow, yet the notion of perfection, or, rather, perfecting, is an essential part of Johnson's concept of happiness. When this and all the other tendencies we have noted are taken into account —that happiness is a complex and dynamic phenomenon involving the exercise of man's highest capabilities as well as his less exalted modes of experience—it appears likely that had Johnson given us a formal definition of happiness, it would be much like

---

[38] One of the most effective arguments from the point of view described in this paragraph is to be found in *Adventurer* No. 111.

[39] *Works*, VI, 73.

the one by Bishop Hooker which he chose as an example for the *Dictionary*:

Happiness is that estate whereby we attain, so far as possibly may be attained, the full possession of that which simply for itself is to be desired, and containeth in it after an eminent sort the contentation of our desires, the highest degree of all our perfection.

Or it would be like that of Cumberland, with which he was also familiar:

I am to advertise the Reader, that by *their Happiness* I here mean their true and intire Happiness; which comprehends all the attainable Perfections both of Mind and Body. . . . Likewise by *those Actions which are suppos'd to be the Means of this Happiness,* I understand, principally, the intire Series of Actions thro' the whole course of Life, which may promote that End.[40]

Thus, a consideration of what Johnson has to say about the nature of happiness tends to confirm Bate's thesis that the legitimate goal of the activity which Johnson constantly insists upon is self realization; but it also raises a rather vexing question—just whose happiness is involved? Bate's apparent purpose is to present those phases of Johnson's wisdom which because of their persisting, universal relevance are the most useful to the modern reader. This purpose his book fulfills admirably. An eighteenth-century reader, however, perhaps because the altruism which so thoroughly permeates our social, political, economic, and moral presuppositions—no matter how rarely it is translated into action—was in his day just winning acceptance, would be curious about the possibility of conflict between the interests of the individual moral agent and the happiness of others. Of course, in the process of turning outward, which Bate sees as essential to the perfecting of the psychological organism, the individual would presumably grow less attentive to his own happiness and more to that of others, but at best this is merely using altruism therapeu-

---

[40] *The Laws of Nature,* p. 269. Maxwell is sometimes awkward, but his is truer to the original than the other English translations.

tically, as a device to benefit oneself. At worst, it is possible to imagine a person perfecting himself—in Bate's terms, achieving a healthy mind—to a considerable degree, without regarding the interests of others, or even at the expense of others. This, as it should be evident from the discussion of his practical ethic, Johnson would regard as vicious.

The eighteenth-century Englishman, made increasingly aware of this dilemma because of the rise of the altruistic spirit, tried to resolve it by proving that self-love and social are really the same. Sometimes, for example, he appealed to the hedonistic impulse: if the greatest of all pleasures is doing good for others, it follows that one best fulfills his obligation to himself by assuming that he has one to the rest of mankind. Johnson was not above pointing out these extra dividends when he sought to persuade his readers to beneficence, but it is obvious that he regarded them merely as inducements, essentially vicarious and but occasionally effective.

In the first place, he says over and over that real beneficence must proceed from principles not feelings. Anyone who bases his beneficence on pleasurable emotion is likely to end as he began, in merely feeling, rather than doing. Secondly, Johnson was positively distrustful of the pleasures of benevolence, so much so that in his personal charity he seems to have sought to counterbalance them by courting ingratitude and unpleasantness.

Another argument, on a higher level, one which Johnson did esteem, derives from the paradoxical nature of the pursuit for happiness. We learn from *Rasselas* that the more strenuously a man pursues happiness the less likely he is to capture it, yet, although happiness is attainable, neither will it come to him who stands and waits. This dilemma, Johnson had resolved ten years before in *The Vanity of Human Wishes*. If one devotes all his energies to striving for virtue, the mind makes the happiness it does not find. However, Johnson was here adapting a classic precept of the pagan moralists of antiquity to a Christian context.

Happiness comes for a large part in that "happier state" referred to at the end of *The Vanity of Human Wishes*. Johnson had too much common sense to suggest, as some did, that pursuing of virtue rather than pleasure will guarantee temporal happiness.

The age's favorite argument for reconciling self-love and social is that first systematically propounded by Cumberland and which in Johnson's thinking takes the form which I have called altruistic utilitarianism. The utilitarian process is obviously inefficient; no specific individual can be sure that his efforts add anything to the general happiness or that the efforts of others will render him happy. But if we accept Johnson's premises that, at best, the political and economic organism can provide only minimal goods —those things without which happiness is impossible——beneficence is certainly the most prudent course for him who seeks his own happiness. It is the way which most directly *tends* toward his happiness in a world where very few expectations are certain of fulfillment.

However, as we have seen in Chapter V, Johnson pushes altruism beyond the point where it can result in any possible benefit for the individual moral agent. If the largest effective social unit is the state and the principle of utility does not function beyond its limits, what practical advantage can he offer his readers to persuade them that they must "love all men"? His concern for the natives of Abyssinia or the Indians of Canada is explained by his own universal compassion, but we cannot account in this way for recurring phrases such as "the great republic of mankind," "the universal league of social beings," and "the great law of mutual benevolence." Clearly, the happiness of others involves values which cannot be completely translated into terms of one's own happiness. In Johnson's moral thought the happiness of others is an end in itself.

We may conclude, then, that although Johnson exhibits a concern with good intentions which is normal to his day and shares with most moralists a faith in the importance of the development of proper habits and sound character, he disagrees with those contemporaries who make morality principally a matter of virtuous character. He does not regard morality as mainly consisting in being goodhearted or in *being* anything, because above all morality to him means *doing*. The chief goals of the activity so fundamental to his moral thinking are the happiness of the agent, which involves self-realization, and the happiness of others.

VII

Morality and Religion

Nothing has been said concerning the third class of ethical system which Johnson mentions in his review of Jenyns's *Free Enquiry,* the sort where morality is regarded primarily as dutiful obedience to law. So far, we have been able to confirm his rejection of morals as a matter of virtuous character and his acceptance of the consequences of an action as the only real criterion of its morality. We could now take at face value his rejection of this third system were it not for the strange paradox which is involved. In the review, one of his very few discussions of ethical theory, he rejects the ethics of duty, but in practice he constantly uses the terminology of this system, words like *law, duty,* and *principles.* What is more surprising, the ethics of duty which he is repudiating means to Johnson, the ethics of religious duty, the notion that good and evil depend "on the will of God," yet no one can read much of Johnson's moral writing without sensing the ultimately religious impetus behind it. If, then, we can resolve this paradox, we ought to be able to solve a problem which concerns impulses so fundamental that it is best left until last: the relation between Johnson's moral notions and his religious professions.

Actually Johnson's frequent references to *law, principle, duty,* and *obligation* could be used to transform completely the conclusions reached in the last chapter. Neither the happiness of others nor personal fulfillment need be regarded as ends in themselves; both may be sought merely because men are obligated to seek them. That this is true with respect to the happiness of others is obvious, since we are accustomed to regarding charity as a duty. It may be less evident with respect to seeking one's own happiness, which at its highest level involves self-realization, because we are equally accustomed to regarding this as an end in itself. Bate's admirable adaptation of Johnson to our needs is achieved by assuming for the purposes of his discussion that Johnson's aims in ministering to the mind are as naturalistic as those of Sigmund Freud. As Bate recognizes, Johnson actually belongs not with the naturalistic moralists but to the older humanistic tradition, and the humanistic moralist, though he often values self-realization for its own sake, usually regards it as instrumental to a higher end or duty. Some secular moralists of antiquity consider self-realization as enabling the individual to serve social ends—Marcus Aurelius exemplifies this in his *Meditations* and in the conduct of his own life. Others regard fulfillment as the process of fitting the individual into some larger, cosmological, pattern. Milton, in his notion that each man by perfecting himself can repair the damage wrought by our original parents and come closer to God, typifies the attitude of the sophisticated religious moralist of the Renaissance toward self-realization.

Of course it would be wrong to ascribe such fundamental significance, even hypothetically, to many of the instances where Johnson uses the terminology of duty ethics. Moralists of all persuasions have made good use of the notion that morality consists in dutiful conformity to some principle, as distinguished from the pursuit of good ends. Suppose, for instance, that Johnson regards personal happiness as the ultimate goal of all moral action. How is he to persuade men to act for their own happiness when this happiness cannot be found but, instead, must be "made" by some action which often is contrary to an immediately pleasurable end? We come again to an example of the important part that Johnson's pessimism plays in shaping his moral notions. He would feel, if for no other reasons, that men need principles backed up by a sense of obligation to guide them to a moral life because they are neither good-natured enough or rational enough to get along without them.

Johnson argued the necessity for principles and laws most forcibly when he found himself confronted with one of those optimists who makes morality depend upon good nature. On July 20, 1763, Johnson supped in Boswell's chambers with George Dempster, a disciple of Hume and Rousseau. Little of what Dempster said upon this occasion has been preserved, but he did maintain that intrinsic merit ought to make the only distinction among mankind, and he must have held forth on the power of man's benevolent instincts, because he provoked Johnson to an outburst which I have referred to before, beginning, "Pity is not natural to man. Children are always cruel. . . ." The next day Johnson was still nettled. When Boswell defended Dempster as one whose principles have been poisoned, but who is, nevertheless, "a benevolent good man," Johnson replied that

we can have no dependence upon that instinctive, that constitutional goodness which is not founded upon principle. I grant you that such a man may be a very amiable member of society. I can conceive him placed in such a situation that he is not much tempted to deviate from what is right; and as every man prefers virtue, when there is not some strong incitement to transgress its precepts, I can conceive him doing nothing wrong. But if such a man stood in need of money, I should not like to trust him.[1]

[1] *Life,* I, 443–444.

And with respect to the weakness of human reason as an argument for principles and the notion of obligation, Johnson feels that even the man who does prefer his ultimate happiness to some present advantage cannot look very far into the future. Imlac tells Nekayah that

> when we act according to our duty, we commit the event to him by whose laws our actions are governed, and who will suffer none to be finally punished for obedience. When, in prospect of some good, whether natural or moral, we break the rules prescribed us, we withdraw from the direction of superiour wisdom, and take all consequences upon ourselves. . . . When we consult only our own policy, and attempt to find a nearer way to good, by overleaping the settled boundaries of right and wrong, we cannot be happy even by success, because we cannot escape the consciousness of our fault; but, if we miscarry, the disappointment is irremediably embittered.[2]

It would be very helpful had Johnson somewhere explained the relation between the Divine ordinances refered to in this passage and the moral law of which he also speaks. Presumably they are identical, the difference lying in the mode of apprehension, for according to Johnson's usual way of speaking the ultimate moral law seems to be available through either reason or revelation—"principles can only be strong, by the strength of understanding, or the cogency of religion."[3] This is not the sort of topic on which anyone who knows Johnson well would expect him to commit himself, and, actually, it matters not for the purposes of the present discussion whether he exactly defines the relation, because he states quite clearly that the obligation to obey the moral law—whatever the law's origin and real nature—is religious: "In moral and religious questions only, a wise man will hold no consultations with fashion, because these duties are constant

---

[2] *Rasselas*, p. 151. See also *Works*, VI, 71 (Review of a *Free Enquiry*).

[3] *Letters*, I, 386. Compare *Doctor Johnson and the English Law*, p. 82. Were more of the Vinerian Lectures available it might be possible to tell more about Johnson's notion of the relation of the two, but it is not likely that he would consider the problem very urgent.

and immutable, and depend not on the notions of men, but the commands of Heaven." [4]

Most of the time when Johnson speaks in terms of duty he is speaking in a religious context, and it is the religious element in his moral notions which must be examined closely if his paradoxical rejection of the ethics of duty is to be understood. He gives several reasons why men must obey divine commands. In various places he says that by obeying divine commands man worships God, he shows his gratitude, and proves his love, but there is no doubt as to the predominant reason: man must obey because if he does not do so he will suffer for it in the future state.[5] Johnson's habitual insistence on this point decisively sets him apart from the mainstream of popular moralizing during his day. The sentimental benevolists, following a line of argument propounded most elegantly by the third Earl of Shaftesbury, professed to determine the morality of actions according to the purity of the motives which gave rise to them. Those motives were considered purest which were most thoroughly other-regarding, or which derived most completely from man's benevolent instincts with the smallest admixture of other passions and appetites. Since hope of reward and fear of punishment are pre-eminently self-regarding emotions, these moralists felt that no action dependent upon them can be truly benevolent or moral. This sort of thinking is in part responsible for the alliance of deism with sentimentalism, which was discussed in the first chapter. Deism, which hoped to free morality from dependence upon revelation, offered the sentimental benevolist the hope of freeing it from self-interest.

Johnson, on the other hand, never hesitates to appeal to reward

[4] *Works,* IV, 138 (*Adventurer* No. 131).

[5] See, for example, *Rambler* Nos. 28, 29, 53, 70, 78, 185; *Idler* No. 43; *Rasselas,* ch. xxxiii; the preface to the *Preceptor;* Review of a *Free Enquiry;* and Sermons II, IV, V, XII, and XIV. The indexes to *Life* and *Letters,* though incomplete, will provide references to Johnson's later utterances to prove that his views did not change as he grew older.

and punishment. Some sort of sanctions are necessary to enforce duty for the same reason that the notions of duty and law are necessary in the first place. Man is neither benevolent enough nor sufficiently rational to act rightly without them.

The laws of mere morality are of no coercive power; and, however they may, by conviction of their fitness, please the reasoner in the shade, when the passions stagnate without impulse, and the appetites are secluded from their objects, they will be of little force against the ardour of desire, or the vehemence of rage, amidst the pleasures and tumults of the world. To counteract the power of temptations, hope must be excited by the prospect of rewards, and fear by the expectation of punishment; and virtue may owe her panegyricks to morality, but must derive her authority from religion.[6]

If the average man were rational enough, he might be able to act in his own, long-term interest without the inducement provided by divine sanctions. The really difficult task is to make him also regard the happiness of others, which, as we have seen, Johnson considers a good of the highest order. Man had to be constituted so as to look out for himself first; were he not, he could not survive. "No man can be obliged by nature, to prefer, ultimately the happiness of others to his own." [7] And since "every man is conscious, that he neither performs, nor forbears any thing upon any other motive than the prospect, either of an immediate gratification, or a distant reward," [8] the great task of each man

is to make the future predominate over the present, to impress upon his mind so strong a sense of the importance of obedience to the divine will, of the value of the reward promised to virtue, and the terrours of the punishment denounced against crimes, as may overbear all the temptations which temporal hope or fear can bring in his way.[9]

Johnson talks this way so often, that it may seem that there

[6] *Works,* V, 243–244 (Preface to the *Preceptor*). Compare this with Dr. Harrison's similar remarks in Fielding's *Amelia,* XII, v, and with *Life,* V, 359–360.

[7] *Works,* VI, 71 (Review of a *Free Enquiry*).

[8] *Works,* IX, 414 (Sermon XIV). See also *Life,* III, 342.

[9] *Works,* II, 31–32 (*Rambler* No. 7) .

could be no question concerning what role religion plays in his moral thinking. However, for two reasons all this evidence does not settle the matter. In the first place, Johnson is intensely conscious of the fact that as a moralist and a public figure he has a responsibility to maintain the proprieties. The eighteenth century had more respect for the force of example than ours does, so much, that it is hard to imagine Johnson as anything but a champion of religion in public, whatever his private convictions might be. Secondly, the bulk of these statements occur in writings specifically moral, and Johnson, because he is a practical moralist, always keeps his eye on the end to be achieved, the action to be shaped. Unlike the ethical philosopher, he has no interest in expounding a unified and consistent body of moral truth. There is the possibility, then, that Johnson's assertions concerning reward and punishment in a future state are largely intended for their therapeutic effect on his readers rather than as an expression of his own eschatological convictions.

Several noted students of Johnson feel that he really does not mean it. Consider, for instance, this statement from Joseph Wood Krutch's valuable *Samuel Johnson*:

The sister of Rasselas has been made to say: "To me the choice of life is become less important; I hope, hereafter, to think only on the choice of eternity," and thus Johnson pays to orthodoxy, as he always does, the tribute of formal profession. But these formal professions cannot mean to him what they would have meant had they been as simply and vividly believed in as some have believed them, and here they constitute only the formal rather than the effective moral. Interpreted in the light of his own life as he lived it, the conclusion of *Candide* ("Let us cultivate our garden") would be almost as appropriate to *Rasselas* and therein, perhaps, lies one of the resemblances between the two books which made champions of English respectability so anxious to labor the obvious differences between them.[10]

I have already suggested that one of the morals of *Rasselas*— especially if the book is "interpreted in the light" of Johnson's

[10] (New York, 1944), p. 183.

own life—is that we are all to cultivate our gardens, although I do not think that the eighteenth-century reader would pass over, as Krutch does, Johnson's important, and un-Voltairean, qualification, that each is to cultivate his garden "by promoting within his circle, however narrow, the happiness of others." It is also easy to agree that the religious moral is but lightly drawn in *Rasselas:* how lightly is evident when the tale is contrasted with many of the periodical essays, with "The Vision of Theodore," *The Vanity of Human Wishes,* the *Sermons,* and with Johnson's private journals. But the suggestion that this omission means that Johnson lacked a vivid belief in the importance of the choice of eternity and that his constant references to reward and punishment are merely formal professions, must be examined further.

It would seem easy enough to test the sincerity of Johnson's continual references to reward and punishment in a future state by comparing them with his personal attitude towards death. No one denies the genuineness of Johnson's own fear of death; he accurately describes his experience when he says that "the secret horrour of the last is inseparable from a thinking being, whose life is limited, and to whom death is dreadful." [11] "The whole of life is but keeping away the thoughts of it." [12] If the references to future punishment which appear in his moral essays are merely formal, there must be some other explanation for his personal terror.

The trouble is that there is no substantial agreement as to why Johnson fears death so. On one of those occasions when Boswell brings up the subject to see how he will react, just as one might worry a chained bear, Johnson lists the possible motives for this fear. Boswell has referred to a passage in Drummond of Hawthornden's "Cypress Grove," "where it is said that the world is a mere show; and that it is unreasonable for man to wish to con-

---

[11] *Works,* IV, 449 (*Idler* No. 103).
[12] *Life,* II, 93.

tinue in the showroom, after he has seen it. Let him go cheerfully out and give space to other spectators." And Johnson replies,

Yes, sir, if he is sure he is to be well, after he goes out of it. But if he is to grow blind after he goes out of the show-room, and never to see any thing again; or if he does not know whither he is to go next, a man will not go cheerfully out of a show-room. No wise man will be contented to die, if he thinks he is to go into a state of punishment. Nay, no wise man will be contented to die, if he thinks he is to fall into annihilation: for however unhappy any man's existence may be, he yet would rather have it, than not exist at all.[13]

Death can be dreaded, then, because the individual fears punishment, or the unknown, or annihilation, or because he loves life, painful as it may be.

A sampling of the opinions of scholars who have studied the subject reveals little uniformity. Krutch, at one place or another in his biography, assigns all four motives to Johnson. He is especially convincing when he discusses the part played by Johnson's zest for life. Jean H. Hagstrum describes Johnson's faith as an orthodox religion of fear, as does Philip Williams, in an admirably judicious and perceptive essay.[14] Watkins also makes a strong case for Johnson's fear of hellfire, and, in addition, believes that he was perturbed by the thought of annihilation.[15] Because Bate feels the need for certitude and control through order and pattern to be one of the primary impulses of Johnson's nature, he emphasizes the fear of annihilation, linking it to the terror of insanity as a loss of control and awareness.[16] For another reason, Ernest C. Mossner also regards annihilation as most significant.[17]

---

[13] *Life*, V, 180.

[14] Jean H. Hagstrum, "On Doctor Johnson's Fear of Death," *ELH*, XIV (1947), 308–319. Philip Williams, "Samuel Johnson's Central Tension: Faith and the Fear of Death," *North Japan College Literary Journal*, Sept. 1958, pp. 1–35. See also *Samuel Johnson's Literary Criticism*, pp. 68–69.

[15] *Perilous Balance*, pp. 56–57.

[16] *The Achievement of Samuel Johnson*, pp. 159–162.

[17] *The Forgotten Hume* (New York, 1943), pp. 203–204.

Stuart Gerry Brown stresses the dread of divine punishment, but feels that the thought of annihilation and Johnson's abhorrence of solitude may have some bearing on the intensity with which he fears death.[18]

Such differences of opinion are easy enough to understand. For one thing, they are in part due to differences of emphasis. No one presumes to determine the exact proportions in which these various impulses react to produce Johnson's intense fear of death. Again, although Johnson does not hesitate to refer to the future state, he is most reluctant to discuss it at any length.

This reluctance, which is sometimes attributed to a fear that there may be no life after death, can be explained without resorting to subtleties. Eschatology is not the only branch of theology which Johnson hesitates to discuss, yet we know from his own statements and from the citations in the *Dictionary,* that he had read widely in theology and could have said much. Piety explains this hesitation better than skepticism does. The *Sermons,* practical divinity, offered Johnson his only opportunity to speak out. Religion is not for the Club, nor is it a proper subject for the periodical essay, prose fiction, biography, or poetry. Furthermore the nature of the future state is the sort of topic which can be discussed only if one is willing to resort to that free speculation which Johnson strongly mistrusted, wherever it was applied.

Even though he avoids discussing the future state, Johnson seems absolutely sure of its existence. This argues strongly that fear of what might happen to him in the afterlife had a large part in shaping his attitude toward death. If it did not, we should certainly find somewhere among his hundreds of public and private references to futurity, one statement which definitely casts doubt on his continuing belief in an afterlife. The best that anyone has been able to bring forward are his frequent doubts about his own salvation, a few references to annihilation, and his uncertainty as to the nature of the future state.

[18] "Dr. Johnson and the Religious Problem," *English Studies,* XX (1938), 1–17.

Johnson feels he has several good reasons for believing in an afterlife. Most important is the authority of revelation, but he also thinks that its existence can be established independently. "One evidence of a future state, is the uncertainty of any present reward for goodness." [19] "However the lot of the good and bad may be huddled together in the seeming confusion of our present state, the time shall undoubtedly come, when the most virtuous will be the most happy." [20] Johnson's favorite variant of this argument is not so artless. It derives from his painful awareness of how little of the human potential can ever be realized, and also from his consciousness of the perpetual gulf between man's ability to desire and his capacity to enjoy, the one boundless and the other circumscribed and insufficient:

The miseries of life may, perhaps, afford some proof of a future state, compared as well with the mercy as the justice of God. It is scarcely to be imagined that infinite Benevolence would create a being capable of enjoying so much more than is here to be enjoyed, and qualified by nature to prolong pain by remembrance, and anticipate it by terrour, if he was not designed for something nobler and better than a state, in which many of his faculties can serve only for his torment; in which he is to be importuned by desires that can never be satisfied, to feel many evils which he had no power to avoid, and to fear many which he shall never feel: there will surely come a time, when every capacity of happiness shall be filled, and none shall be wretched but by his own fault.[21]

If a source need be found for this line of reasoning, Johnson was certainly familiar with Hooker's eloquent use of it.

For man doth not seem to rest satisfied, either with fruition of that wherewith his life is preserved, or with the performance of such actions as advance him most deservedly in estimation; but doth further covet, yea oftentimes manifestly pursue with great sedulity and earnest-

---

[19] *Works*, II, 254 (*Rambler* No. 52).

[20] *Works*, VI, 72 (Review of a *Free Enquiry*).

[21] *Works*, IV, 122 (*Adventurer* No. 120). See also IV, 260 (*Idler* No. 37); IX, 348 (Sermon VI); IX, 403 (Sermon XII); *Lives*, III, 418–419 (Akenside); and *Letters*, II, 251.

ness, that which cannot stand him in any stead or vital use. . . . For although the beauties, riches, honours, sciences, virtues, and perfections of all men living, were in the present possession of one; yet somewhat beyond and above all this there would still be sought and earnestly thirsted for. So that Nature even in this life doth plainly claim and call for a more divine perfection.[22]

Most of those who minimize Johnson's fear of eternal punishment tend to ignore the fact that he toyed with the heterodox notion of a middle state immediately preceding the future one, yet there is abundant evidence that he was much attracted by this idea. In the epitaph, *Orate pro anima miserimmi peccatoris* he felt that "there was nothing trifling or ludicrous, nothing that did not tend to the noblest end, the propagation of piety, and the increase of devotion."[23] And against Hawkins's attempt to explain away the impression that Johnson considered the doctrine of purgatory as true in addition to useful, may be weighed the testimony of Boswell, who appears himself to have been won over to the belief before he died.[24] Furthermore, Johnson's credulity regarding apparitions and other evidences of the world of spirits, ought to have embarrassed Johnsonians of his day and ours less than it has, because it is in part based on the sound, albeit nonjuring doctrine that a total disbelief of apparitions "is adverse to the opinion of the existence of the soul between death and the last day."[25] Here Johnson's reasoning is like that of Archibald Campbell, author of *The Doctrines of a Middle State between Death and the Resurrection* (1721), a book which Johnson owned and which he recommended on that memorable day when he visited a relative of Campbell's, the Duke of Argyle.[26] Finally, there is the testimony of Johnson's prayers—sometimes conditional, sometimes not—for the departed spirits of his father

[22] *Ecclesiastical Polity*, I, xi, 4.
[23] *Works*, V, 264 (Essay on Epitaphs).
[24] Hawkins's *Life*, pp. 448–451; Boswell's *Life*, I, 240–241, and V, 562.
[25] *Life*, IV, 94. He was also fond of the notion of guardian spirits. See *Life*, I, 236, and *Letters*, I, 35.
[26] See p. xvii of Campbell's treatise.

and mother, his brother, of Tetty, of Bathhurst, and of Henry Thrale. In the light of all this evidence that Johnson went so far beyond the Anglican norm in his attitude toward purgatory, it is very difficult to conceive of him as having a weaker-than-average faith in the existence of a future state.

As we have seen, Johnson refuses to speculate on what the future state may be like, beyond the fact that it can involve either indefinable joys or punishments.[27] "Revelation is not wholly silent" but it can tell us no more than this. "Reason deserts us at the brink of the grave, and can give no further intelligence." [28] Because Johnson's fears are so impressively real, one is sometimes tempted to believe that he looked forward to roasting in a Hell constructed according to specifications drawn up by a medieval homilist. However, this is to assume a Johnson less humble and far more naive than the evidence allows. He feels that reason is not competent to pronounce on the afterlife because of the radical discontinuity between this state and the next. What is to come is like nothing he has ever known and nothing he can conceive. Part of Johnson's fear is fear of the unknown.

Surely, nothing can so much disturb the passions, or perplex the intellects of man, as the disruption of his union with visible nature; a separation from all that has hitherto delighted or engaged him; a change not only of the place, but the manner of his being; an entrance into a state not simply which he knows not, but which perhaps he has not faculties to know; an immediate and perceptible communication with the supreme Being, and, what is above all distressful and alarming, the final sentence, and unalterable allotment.[29]

Johnson's frequent statements in this vein often embarrassed and perplexed his admirers, for even the damaging admission that his piety was unfashionably tinged with enthusiasm could not satisfactorily account for the intensity of his fear and feelings

[27] See, for instance, Life, II, 162–163; III, 200; and IV, 279–280, 299–300; also Letters, I, 30, and Lives, I, 181 (Milton).

[28] Works, IV, 272 (Idler No. 41).

[29] Works, II, 367–368 (Rambler No. 78).

of guilt. Boswell and Hawkins try to supply the guilt by hinting at youthful indiscretions. Robert Anderson, another biographer, blames Johnson's anxieties on Calvinistic prejudices absorbed at an early age. This hypothesis, which has been echoed by some later writers, involves a fallacy, as Johnson himself points out:

> Some people are not afraid, because they look upon salvation as the effect of an absolute decree, and think they feel in themselves the marks of sanctification. Others, and those the most rational in my opinion, look upon salvation as conditional; and as they never can be sure that they have complied with the conditions, they are afraid.[30]

But during his own century, the attitude of the majority of Johnson's admirers is summed up in Fanny Burney's bewildered question, "Good and excellent as he is, how can he so fear death?" and their overinsistence on his purity of life must have sprung from a concern that his fears might be misinterpreted.

Occasionally, Johnson's torments were aggravated by the fear that perhaps annihilation instead of an afterlife awaited him. He found little comfort in the old Epicurean maxim that, since we can have no subjective experience of annihilation, it is foolish to fear death. When Anna Seward, The Swan of Lichfield, sought to press this argument on him, he retorted, "Mere existence is so much better than nothing, that one would rather exist even in pain, than not exist . . ." and, a little while later, "The lady confounds annihilation, which is nothing, with the apprehension of it, which is dreadful." [31] Here Johnson reveals the source of this particular dread, his consuming thirst for life, which is liable to escape the attention of the casual observer of his pessimistic habit of speech when moralizing, his physical and mental torments, and his frequent thralldom to lethargy. In a letter to Bennet Langton, he wrote, "I have risen every morning since Newyears day at about eight, when I was up, I have indeed done but little, yet it is no slight advancement to obtain for so many hours

[30] *Life*, IV, 278.
[31] *Life*, III, 295–296.

more the consciousness of being." [32] And he even transferred his own emotions to members of the animal kingdom. "There is much talk of the misery which we cause to the brute creation; but they are recompensed by existence." [33]

Because a state of eternal punishment is at least a state of being, Johnson found the thought of it more bearable than the apprehension of not being.[34] Nevertheless, to say that Johnson preferred eternal torment to annihilation is not to suggest that the latter rather than the former was the chief reason for his horror of death. This suggestion is of recent date; none of those who knew him so well even hint at such a thing. There are literally hundreds of references to futurity in Johnson's writings and conversation and but a handful to annihilation. Furthermore, some of the passages brought forward today as evidence of his fear of annihilation did not in Johnson's more pious era imply anything more than an orthodox, but perhaps too fervid, belief in conditional salvation.[35]

Modern students of Johnson who have examined his fear of annihilation vary greatly in their opinions of how much it contributed to his general terror of death. Even the most devout believer may at time suffer misgivings with respect to the immortality of the soul, and Watkins and S. G. Brown seem to feel, as I do, that Johnson's doubts are just an occasional phenomenon. W. J. Bate goes further and makes a strong case for a relation between Johnson's fear of death, his insomnia, and his horror of insanity. He suggests that "the most drastic compulsion of Johnson, . . . is that of reason itself—the compulsion to be fully and finally aware." [36]

Only one phase of Bate's argument runs counter to what has

---

[32] *Letters*, I, 185.
[33] *Life*, III, 53.
[34] *Life*, III, 294–296; V, 180.
[35] See Jean H. Hagstrum, "On Doctor Johnson's Fear of Death," *ELH*, XIV (1947), 308–319.
[36] *The Achievement of Samuel Johnson*, p. 162.

been said in this chapter. This is the suggestion—he does not seem to insist—that the only alternative to actual fire and brimstone is annihilation, and that, because millions of orthodox Anglicans shared Johnson's faith without experiencing his terror, the terror is best explained as the result of an unorthodox belief in annihilation. It seems to me that this reasoning tends to oversimplify Johnson's religious ideas, ignoring as it does his constant awareness of the radical disjunction between the realm of the flesh and that of the spirit. Johnson's chief criticism of the Hell of *Paradise Lost* is that Milton mixes his terms, and, ultimately, much of his distaste for religious poetry in general derives from his awareness of disjunction and consequent rejection of anthropomorphism. Johnson is absolutely certain that the afterlife will be a radically different state, involving the annihilation of all he has ever known—this in itself is a powerful motive for fear. Another possible weakness of this sort of reasoning is that, even if it is wise to deduce anything at all about such a *rara avis* as Johnson on the basis of the reactions of the multitude, his fear and trembling, though uncommon to the circles in which he moved, was not such a rare phenomenon during his century. It was, of course, more common to seventeenth-century English piety, and, as Watkins remarks, Johnson was "like a man from another age."

A contrast to Bate's cautious exposition are the extreme interpretations of Johnson's fear of annihilation advanced by Mossner[37] and Krutch,[38] especially that of Mossner, who maintains that Johnson feared death because he equated it with absolute extinction, and who regards this dominant anxiety as shaping Johnson's personality and, above all, his prejudices. The weakness of this premise that Johnson is dominated consciously, or unconsciously, by a simple fear of extinction is that it leaves us with no way of explaining his attitude toward time.

It is to be expected that anyone who abhors death as a species

[37] *The Forgotten Hume*, pp. 204–207.
[38] *Samuel Johnson*, pp. 547–550.

of annihilation will have occasion to grieve for time past. He may well lament chances for pleasure or fulfillment which were missed, or he may long for those experiences which were once enjoyed but never can be again, or he may just feel homesick for the past. Usually, however, if the past is attractive, it is so because it offers him an escape, an opportunity to turn his eyes away from what is to come; if it disturbs him, it does so because the past is the measure of how little time remains. The real focus of his apprehensions lies in the future.

With Johnson, the case is different. To be sure, his fear concerns what is to come, but this fear is closely bound up with tormenting regret for his past life. Indeed, it is his obvious remorse for the past which has given his readers, then and now, the clearest and most disturbing insight into the depths of his agony concerning the future. His remorse has been all the more convincing because it becomes intenser in his more private utterances. The *Prayers and Meditations* is one long, pathetic lamentation for wasted yesterdays. Johnson differs, too, from our hypothetical infidel in that he thinks of time, especially in his more introspective moments, not as hours, and days or years, but as opportunities for work, opportunities which have been or may be profitably used or wasted. He was most of his life haunted by Christ's words, "I must work the works of him that sent me, while it is day: the night cometh when no man can work." He cites this, his favorite Biblical quotation, as early as *Adventurer* No. 120, and he once had part of it engraved on the dial plate of his watch. The way in which Johnson's apprehensions concerning the future seem to stem from the past, cannot be explained at all, if he is assumed to be fundamentally a believer in annihilation who has no really genuine fear of punishment in the future state.

It should be possible at this point to evaluate the part played by reward and punishment in Johnson's moral thinking, but an impediment remains. Johnson's eschatological notions are only a side issue to many modern scholars; behind their reluctance to

grant him belief in a future state lies the conviction that he
was not at heart a devout man. No one accuses him of being a
hypocrite, yet some do feel that Johnson had to fight a constant,
though generally successful battle against his own tendency to
doubt the fundamental truths of religion, that temperamentally
he was better fitted to be a freethinker than a Christian, and that
this dichotomy is a major source of tension in his personality.
Obviously, it would be presumptuous to go further before considering the evidence adduced for his skepticism.

These scholars usually depend on one of four different arguments, or some combination thereof. A few resort to probing
deeply into Johnson's psyche; one cites the hints of Johnson's
contemporaries; some reason that his faith would have been more
placid had it been strong; and others argue by extrapolation that,
because Johnson was a skeptic in some areas, he must have been
one in religion, too. To the first sort of argument there is no
satisfactory reply. This is not the place to ponder the degree to
which religious impulses are primitive to our natures, and since
the essential religiosity even of saints cannot be successfully defended against the assaults of a halfway competent Freudian,
there is no use in arguing Johnson's religious temperament at
this level. All that can be considered here is whether the other
three arguments invalidate the general impression which has
persisted up to our time, that Johnson was as pious as the average
Anglican of his day, if not more so. I do not think they do.

Mossner feels that he has contemporary authority for his thesis
that "Johnson hated Hume because he recognized in him a kindred spirit," because he was himself possessed by a "religious
skepticism, subdued but never extinguished." [39] If any of Johnson's contemporaries believed this to be true, they kept their
views private, at least during his lifetime. The earliest remark

[39] *The Forgotten Hume,* p. 206. For an opposing view of Johnson and Hume,
see Stuart Gerry Brown's "Dr. Johnson and the Religious Problem," *English
Studies,* XX (1938), 1–17, 67.

in this vein which I have been able to find is made by Sir James Mackintosh (1765–1832) in his *Memoirs:*—it should be noted that this Scottish Whig was seventeen when Johnson died:

From the refinements of abstruse speculation he was withheld, partly perhaps by that repugnance to such subtleties which much experience often inspires, and partly also by a secret dread that they might disturb those prejudices in which his mind had found repose from the agitations of doubt.[40]

The only contemporary recognition of Johnson's repressed religious skepticism which Mossner cites was not published until 1855:

A very old gentleman, who had known Johnson intimately, assured me that the bent of his mind was decidedly towards skepticism; that he was literally afraid to examine his own thoughts on religious matters; and that hence partly arose his hatred of Hume and other such writers.[41]

The old gentleman quoted may well have known Johnson and thus have been the only true contemporary of Johnson who both noticed and recorded this religious skepticism. Even if he was, the evidence is third hand, for the "me" of the passage is not Richard Porson, as Mossner states, but his friend William Maltby. In the "Porsoniana," Porson is referred to in the third person, except in those passages which are enclosed in quotes, and this one is not. Accordingly, the provenance of the *locus classicus* for Johnson's religious skepticim is not very reassuring as to its authenticity. Maltby died at the age of ninety-one the year before the "Porsoniana" was published, and it must have been many years earlier that the anonymous "old gentleman" made the observation to him. Later Maltby repeated the remark while "in conversation" with Alexander Dyce, and still later Dyce inserted it in his edition of Rogers's *Table Talk*.

---

[40] *Memoirs of the Life of the Right Honorable Sir James Mackintosh,* ed. Robert James Mackintosh (1836), II, 171.
[41] From "Porsoniana," in *Recollections of the Table Talk of Samuel Rogers* (New York, 1856), p. 326.

Against this tenuous evidence for Johnson's skepticism must be weighed a veritable mountain of contemporary testimony to the solidity of his faith. Because the pattern of our interest in Johnson is so different from that of his eighteenth-century readers, and because he was lax in attending church and in observing some other religious forms, we are often prone to overlook the fact that in his own day Johnson was considered a bulwark of religion and a model of piety. Sir Joshua Reynolds's statement that the Christian religion was with Johnson "such a certain and established truth, that he considered it as a kind of profanation to hold any argument about its truth," [42] and Mrs. Piozzi's conviction that Johnson was "one of the most zealous and pious" Christians "our nation ever produced" [43] are typical of those who admired him most and knew him best.

Perhaps the bias of his friends, however well they knew him, discredits their testimony. If so, we can go to the other extreme and consider the attitude of Soame Jenyns, who cannot be accused of the same sort of bias, and who, if he did not know Johnson intimately, could at least be counted on to magnify any discreditable scrap of information which came his way. But, along with Johnson's friends, he readily admitted the moralist's piety:

> Here lies Sam Johnson:—Reader, have a care
> Tread lightly, lest you wake a sleeping Bear,
> Religious, moral, generous, and humane
> He was; but self-sufficient, proud, and vain,
> Fond of, and overbearing in dispute,
> A Christian, and a Scholar—but a Brute.[44]

So often was this devoutness proclaimed, that another opponent, Anna Seward, protested, "They seek to make Johnson a saint." [45]

The publication of biographies by Hawkins and Boswell did nothing to detract from the popular image of Johnson as a godly

[42] *Misc.*, II, 225.
[43] *Misc.*, I, 158.
[44] *Works* (1790), I, 222. This provoked Boswell to reply with an epitaph on Jenyns.
[45] *Letters* (1811–1813), I, 135.

individual, nor did the *Prayers and Meditations,* despite their enthusiastic tinge and the revelation of Johnson's agonized sense of guilt. The consensus of the next generation is expressed not by the anonymous very old gentleman, but by Nathan Drake (1766–1836):

Whatever may be thought of the speculative reveries of Johnson with regard to immaterial agency, there can be but one opinion as to his piety, sincerity, and, in the privacy of prayer, his thorough humility and contrition. He had a perpetual struggle against morbid sensation, constitutional indolence, and strong appetites; and how well he succeeded in the contest must be apparent to all who shall view his life in the pages of Mr. Boswell, or open his Prayers and Meditations; if not a happy, he was, assuredly, a truly good and pious, man.[46]

Drake is relatively temperate and judicious. Upon reading some of the eulogies of Johnson's piety, even the most confirmed Johnsonian can feel sympathy with Becky Sharp when she hurls "the late revered Doctor's" volume back into the garden of Miss Pinkerton's academy for young ladies.

Thus, to argue for Johnson's religious skepticism on the basis of contemporary authority is in Imlac's words to "set hypothetical possibility against acknowledged certainty." But most of those who believe that Johnson's faith was insecure point rather to the fact that Johnson was tormented by his religion, or to his skepticism in other areas of experience. This passage from Bertrand Bronson's "Johnson Agonistes" provides an example of the first of these arguments:

It is hard to believe, in the face of his intellectual habit and what he says about reasons, that Johnson was naturally religious, or that it would not have been much easier, temperamentally, for him to have been a skeptic. His violence about it is the measure of the desperate fight which it cost him to hold fast his religion. The mind that is predisposed to religion feels itself adrift until it comes to anchor in the harbour of a firm and happy faith.[47]

---

[46] *Essays, Biographical, Critical, and Historical, Illustrative of the Rambler, Adventurer, and Idler* (1809), I, 470.

[47] *Johnson Agonistes and other Essays* (Cambridge, 1946), p. 41.

Bronson may accurately describe the temper of modern religion when he makes a predisposition to it dependent upon the individual's ability to find peace of mind through faith, but it seems to me that if this criterion is insisted upon with respect to antique patterns of piety, it fallaciously restricts the possible varieties of religious experience. One hates to think that John Donne, Richard Baxter, and many other seventeenth-century divines who never came to anchor, were not naturally religious. And Johnson himself warns against ingenuous and "precipitate trust in God":

Trust in God, that trust to which perfect peace is promised, is to be obtained only by repentence, obedience, and supplication, not by nourishing in our own hearts a confused idea of the goodness of God, or by a firm persuasion that we are in a state of grace; by which some have been deceived, as it may be feared, to their own destruction. We are not to imagine ourselves safe, only because we are not harassed with those anxieties about our future state with which others are tormented, but which are so far from being proofs of reprobation, that though they are often mistaken by those that languish under them, they are more frequently evidences of piety, and a sincere and fervent desire of pleasing God.[48]

In Johnson's view, anxiety, while it is no guarantee that one is saved, is natural to the truly pious man, because he cannot partake of that confidence which is to be enjoyed at the extremes, whether it derives from the optimism characteristic of the deist and his fellows, or from that righteous assurance of election common to strong Calvinists.

The ideas in this passage, which are repeated again and again in the *Sermons* and in those moral essays which deal with religion, give the key to the nature of Johnson's piety. They explain, for instance, the true significance of those doubts and scruples that are so often expressed in the pages of the *Prayers and Meditations*. A number of these expressions which were deleted by George Strahan, to whom Johnson entrusted publication of the

[48] *Works*, IX, 421–422 (Sermon XIV). See also IX, 409 (Sermon XIII).

manuscript, have been recovered by the editors of the volume for the Yale edition, but the deletions are apparently identical in character with that which was retained and offer no corroboration for the modern suspicion that some of these doubts involve the fundamental truth of Christianity. Strahan apparently reduced the number of these expressions because he feared that readers of the book might consider Johnson's scrupulosity as evidence that he had been a notable sinner at one time or another—and Strahan's fears proved to be justifiable. Actually, those of his contemporaries who did misinterpret Johnson's scruples are not to blame, because, in the first place, Johnson's brand of piety had long since gone out of fashion in his circle; and, secondly, because, aside from a very few cases where he is concerned about his normal propensity to speculate on the Christian mysteries, all of the scruples whose nature is specified bear directly on his worthiness to be saved.[49]

Johnson's doubts regarding his salvation take two forms. The first sort, which are more likely to embarrass the reader than excite his compassion, involve fear that he will be punished for not accomplishing some task—putting his books in order, say— which he has set himself in order to prove that he can overcome his indolence. Sometimes these fears concern small matters indeed, and Johnson seems to be a living illustration of his own definition of *scrupulosity,* as "a minute and nice doubtfulness." However, in the other variety, which he calls Baxter's scruple, is epitomized all the anxious torment which Johnson's religion cost him. Richard Baxter described his scruple as the doubt that he had sufficient faith to merit salvation, and some of the causes he listed for it illuminate Johnson's case. He asked why he still was so immersed in the flesh; he "found more Fear than Love" in his duty; and he could not understand how any one who had

---

[49] Among his close friends, Mrs. Piozzi seems to understand the nature of his scruples best. *Misc.,* I, 224 (Anecdotes). Williams discusses the attitudes of Johnson's friends very thoroughly in his "Samuel Johnson's Central Tension."

saving grace could go on sinning *"upon knowledge and delibera-tion,"* be the sins "never so small." [50]

Is the element of anguish and struggle in Johnson's religious experience, typified by these scruples, a sign of weak faith or evidence that his temperament is better suited to free thinking? Johnson answers that question when he remarks that the scruple is "its own confutation." This is one of those thoughts which when applied subjectively offer little comfort, but which are none the less true, objectively considered. Those of weak faith, those who are not in some degree naturally disposed to piety, seldom suffer from Baxter's scruple. In the passage just cited from the fourteenth Sermon Johnson argued that anxiety is not necessarily an indication of sufficient faith; more frequently, as in *Rambler* No. 110, he states the corollary proposition that peace of mind in a Christian is likely to mean that his conviction is not strong enough:

If he who considers himself as suspended over the abyss of eternal perdition only by the thread of life, which must soon part by its own weakness, and which the wing of every minute may divide, can cast his eyes round him without shuddering with horrour, or panting with security; what can he judge of himself, but that he is not yet awakened to sufficient conviction.[51]

Accordingly, Johnson is uneasy whenever he deems that his meditations are not sufficiently disquieting:

I perceive an insensibility and heaviness upon me. I am less than commonly oppressed with the sense of sin, and less affected with the shame of Idleness. Yet I will not despair. I will pray to God for resolution, and will endeavour to strengthen my faith in Christ by commemorating his death.[52]

"Faith in proportion to fear," Johnson wrote on a blank leaf of a journal; the one he measured by the other.

[50] *Reliquiae Baxterianae* (1696), pp. 6–7.
[51] *Works*, III, 23. Compare this with Baxter's remarks on p. 7 of the *Reliquiae Baxterianae.*
[52] *Misc.*, I, 29.

It should be remarked in this connection that the practice of reading the *Prayers and Meditations* as a diary of Johnson's day-to-day religious experience tends to exaggerate the element of struggle and pain. He may have suffered such torments daily, but one may hope not. At least, according to the dates of the entries in these journals, we need not assume that he did. Most of them were made on his own birthday, on the anniversary of his wife's death, on New Year's Day, or during the Easter season, and the bulk of the remaining entries commemorate either the death of someone he loved, the beginning of a new endeavor, or some other event that was very important to him. There seems to be good reason to suppose that these meditations are just as much religious exercises as the fasts he sometimes observed, that they are periods of heightened introspection and sensibility, consciously entered into after the fashion of the previous century, in the hope of renewing the motives to piety and virtue.

Sorrow and fear, and anxiety, are properly not parts, but adjuncts of repentance; yet they are too closely connected with it to be easily separated; for they not only mark its sincerity, *but promote its efficacy*.[53]

Fear is also functional.

Most of those who point to Johnson's fears as the mark of an insecure faith seem to feel that much of his anxiety stems from a concern lest his faith be overcome by that fundamentally skeptical cast of mind which shows itself in his attitude toward almost every other aspect of experience. He is a skeptic in all else, hence, he must have some tendency to be a skeptic in this. In other words, if Johnson let himself go, he might well turn into a deist. It hardly benefits anyone to pronounce categorically where such antinomies are involved. Certainly, as Bate remarks, "to create

---

[53] *Works*, III, 23 (*Rambler* No. 110). My italics. In his essay "On Johnson's Fear of Death," Jean H. Hagstrum points out that Dr. Robert South (1634–1716), of whom Johnson thought highly, insists that this type of self-examination is necessary to salvation.

a clean-cut two-dimensional alternative between 'doubt' or 'belief,' and then apply either singly, is a rather simple-minded procedure"; yet, I feel that part of the disagreement surrounding this whole question can be traced specifically to a confusion of terms, *skepticism* and *freethinking.* The two mean more or less the same thing today, and many skeptics of the past have been freethinkers, but to equate the terms when speaking of seventeenth or eighteenth-century English, is to put oneself in the position of the American who upon encountering Continental anticlericalism, can only judge it on the basis of his own experience and accordingly equates it with anticatholicism.

Johnson's skepticism manifests itself in two principal ways, both of which illustrate his empirical habit of thought, which I discussed in the first chapter. For one thing, he is incredulous with respect to particular facts. This warning to Joseph Warton is typical of his attitude:

I cannot forbear to hint to this writer, and all others, the danger and weakness of trusting too readily to information. Nothing but experience could evince the frequency of false information, or enable any man to conceive, that so many groundless reports should be propagated, as every man of eminence may hear of himself. Some men relate what they think, as what they know; some men, of confused memories and habitual inaccuracy, ascribe to one man, what belongs to another; and some talk on, without thought or care.[54]

But this is an inquiring sort of incredulity. Johnson is incredulous because he knows that the mass of available false information, stemming largely, as it does, from fatuity rather than knavery, is virtually boundless and poses a constant threat to anyone who, like himself, possesses that insatiable appetite for accurate particulars which one sees reflected in the pages of *A Journey to the Western Islands*[55] or in Johnson's experiments to determine the rate at which his fingernails grow.

[54] *Works,* VI, 42 (Review of an *Essay on the Writings and Genius of Pope*).
[55] See, for example, p. 133.

Complementary to this, is a more general skepticism directed against those forms of knowledge which Johnson considers to be the products of human presumption. Although he speculated occasionally, as is shown by the remorse he sometimes expresses in the *Prayers and Meditations* for his musings about divine mysteries, no one who has maintained that Johnson had a metaphysical turn of mind, has been able to point to any fruits of this propensity. The closest Johnson comes to being metaphysical in any legitimate sense of the word is when he is chastising Soame Jenyns for his metaphysical efforts, and, as repugnant as some of Jenyns's specific conclusions are to Johnson, they do not annoy him as much as the fact that Jenyns attempted to determine such matters. Johnson's skepticism concerning speculative knowledge does not derive from a fear that false knowledge will drive out true; rather, it is the product of his feeling of nescience, his conviction that man can only have real assurance regarding what has some firm basis in the senses or what God has chosen to reveal to him, and that between these two areas of certainty lies a void about which he can know little, in his present state.

It seems to me that to insist that these two sorts of skepticism imply that Johnson's faith was fundamentally insecure, is to misunderstand the peculiar dilemma of the orthodoxly pious, thoughtful man of his time. Actually, Johnson's skepticism argues the strength of his faith. Neither is it related, even remotely, to free thinking, nor is it much like the skepticism of the seventeenth century, so ably described by Margaret L. Wiley in *The Subtle Knot*.[56] The pious man of the eighteenth century could not let his imagination and reason range free to mediate between the realms of the flesh and the spirit in an ever-widening pattern of doubt and discovery. Professor Wiley's disappointment with the eighteenth century for abandoning a method of insight which greatly enriched human experience, in favor of more pedestrian ways of knowing, a constricted horizon, and a simplified version

[56] (Cambridge, Mass., 1952).

of truth, is easy to understand. Yet, among the various forces which brought about this shift in the mode of seeking truth—indeed, in the concept of what sort of truth is worth seeking—none had more impact upon the orthodox religionist than the growth of deism, which had its source in the confluence of two streams of thought each owing much to the skeptical approach to truth, the rational theology of Lord Herbert of Cherbury and the empiricism of Bacon and Hobbes. At first, deism depended upon a concept of reason which involved both innate ideas and intuitionism, but by the early decades of the eighteenth century it is hard to find a deist whose epistemology is not that of Locke and who does not subscribe to the pedestrian concept of reason which I describe in the first chapter. When the deist seeks to erect on a footing of empirical clay a structure intended to reach to the world of the spirit, he is not likely to get far off the ground, and, what is especially disturbing to the orthodox, he is not likely to realize how far short of the mark his structure stands.

Now how is the pious and thoughtful man who has himself accepted the Lockean epistemology to react to this situation? I think the answer is obvious. As Meyrick Carre has noted, during the early part of the century the orthodox religionist often brings a new sort of skepticism to bear upon the end-product of the old. He uses the Lockean restrictions upon the rational faculty, as an argument against the deists, very much as Bacon had used empirical principles to undermine scholastic rational theology.[57] He reaffirms Bacon's principle "that sacred theology must be drawn from the word and oracles of God; not from the light of nature, or the dictates of reason."[58] However negative and nescient this sort of skepticism may be, it allows a man a richer spiritual life and more capacity for wonder than deism does, and it is likely to be stronger as his faith is stronger.

[57] For some specific examples of the use of Lockean epistemology by the orthodox, see John W. Yolton's illuminating study *John Locke and the Way of Ideas* (Oxford, 1956), pp. 181–202.

[58] *De augmentis,* IX.

Above all, this fideistic skepticism should not be confused with the freethinking variety. Hagstrum makes this clear in his concise and penetrating discussion of Johnson's religious beliefs: "skepticism about a personal, judging God or about the accountability of man . . . might have given him some measure of the comfort that he, as a victim of his own kind of faith, was never able to attain." [59] All men may be compounded of opposites, yet the trait most characteristic of the temperament genuinely disposed to freethinking is assurance, not agony.

I hope this long digression into the subject of Johnson's religious beliefs and his fear of death has made it clear why I cannot accept the theory that his distress results for the most part from insecure faith and a terror of annihilation, rather than from a temperament emotionally disposed to religion and from a positive concern for salvation. And, if I am right in rejecting this theory, it follows that Johnson constantly alludes to reward and punishment in a future state not because it is expected of him, not merely because he hopes thereby to induce his readers to do right, but because fear of future punishment is fundamental to his moral notions.

He certainly does know that neither religious faith nor morality ought to depend predominantly on fear. For instance, when the Duc de Chalnes remarked to him "that the morality of the different religions existing in the world was nearly the same," he replied, "but you must acknowledge, my lord, . . . that the Christian religion alone puts it upon its proper basis—the fear and love of God." [60] And he usually phrases his prayers so as to emphasize the notion of obligation rather than concern for his own fate: "grant that the time which thou shalt yet afford me may be spent to thy glory, and the salvation of my own Soul." "Thy will" usually comes before "my salvation." Yet, given his conviction of his own unworthiness and his clear insight into the weaknesses

[59] "On Doctor Johnson's Fear of Death," *ELH*, XIV (1947), 318. For a very well-documented and more extensive discussion of the subject see Philip Williams's "Samuel Johnson's Central Tension," cited above.

[60] *Misc.*, II, 307.

of all men, it is not surprising that the notion of divine sanctions becomes central to Johnson's moral thought and that we never find him worrying, as Baxter does, that there is more fear than love in his duty.

I think we are now in a position to resolve the paradox which I pointed out at the beginning of this chapter, that, although Johnson considers the consequences of an action as more significant than the fact that it may have been done in conformity to some divine ordinance, he in practice refers constantly to duty and law, and he seems to consider that morality is ultimately based on religion. In the first place, it should be kept in mind that when Johnson puts doing good ahead of being dutiful or developing a virtuous character, he is not repudiating these latter criteria, because so far as the practical moralist is concerned, choosing among the three is only a matter of stressing one more than the other two. What Johnson does is to treat virtue and duty as instrumental to ends. We have already seen in the last chapter that consequences are the ultimate criterion and self-interest is the most effective motivation, if Johnson's moral notions are considered from a purely secular point of view. When a man obeys the great law of mutual benevolence by being directly altruistic and, through working to the best of his capability, is indirectly so, he does that which according to utilitarian principles is most likely to benefit himself here. So it is with the religious phase of Johnson's moral system. It is a man's duty to act beneficently, and the good of others is an end in itself, but the individual does his duty because, if he does not, he will suffer the consequences hereafter. Thus the secular and religious phases of the system complement each other neatly, for, if the utilitarian principle fails a specific individual, as often it must, those same activities which merely tended to render him happy in a present state, will assure his happiness in a future one. As Johnson puts it, "to the instructions of infinite wisdom, it was necessary that infinite power should add penal sanctions. That every man . . . to whom these instructions shall be imparted, may know, that he can never, ultimately, injure himself by benefiting others, or, ultimately, by injuring others benefit himself." [61] Virtue for virtue's sake may please the reasoner in the shade, and the Calvinist, assured of his salvation, may be able to act for the sake of duty, but it was the consequences which most impressed Johnson, and it was these which he stressed to his readers.

I must admit that at one time I envisioned the religious aspects of Johnson's moral thinking as more sophisticated, more in accord with the subtlety of thought and perception which one often encounters on other levels of his system. It was some compensation, however, a short while after I decided that my conclusions were inescapable, to come across what I think is the only eighteenth-century attempt to analyze Johnson's moral notions systematically in the context of his times, and in that essay to find my conclusions confirmed. In the "History of the Science of Morals," which appeared in the third edition of the *Encyclopaedia Britannica* (1797), Johnson is described as one of the leading members of a school of moralists which includes Cumberland, Puffendorf, Berkeley, and many others, among them, Soame Jenyns. Among other characteristics of Johnson which we have considered, the author points out that these moralists are utilitarians because they regard virtuous conduct as "that which is naturally productive of the greatest sum of human happiness." And with respect to the religious phase of their system, he says that

the philosophers of this school define virtue to be "the doing good to mankind, in obedience to the will of God, and for the sake of everlasting happiness": So that with them "the good of mankind" is the *subject*, "the will of God" the *criterion* or *rule*, and "everlasting happiness" the *motive*, of human virtue. The moral sense, supposing it real, they consider as a very inadequate rule of conduct. . . . The other rules,

<hr />

[61] *Works,* VI, 71–72 (Review of a *Free Enquiry*). See also *Works,* II, 31–32 (*Rambler* No. 7); II, 136–137 (*Rambler* No. 185); IV, 276 (*Idler* No. 43); IX, 300 (Sermon I); and IX, 322–323 (Sermon IV).

such as the *fitness of things,* abstract *right,* the *truth of things,* the *law of reason,* &c. they consider either as unintelligible, or as relative to some end by which the rules themselves must be tried. . . .

According to this scheme of morals, which rests all obligation on private happiness, the whole difference between an act of *prudence,* and an act of *duty,* is this: That in the former case we consider only what we shall gain or lose in this world; in the latter, what we shall gain or lose in the world to come.[62]

Actually it was foolish of me to repine at the heterogeneous character of what took shape when I began to investigate Johnson's moral system or at the simplicity of what I finally concluded were its bases, for as one becomes more accustomed to looking at his system in the light of the problems of Johnson's day rather than with respect to our own needs, those qualities which at first seemed to recommend it least are seen to be the source of its success. During an era of remarkable transitions in religious, psychological, and moral concepts, Johnson steered a course between those extremes which rendered so many contemporary theories ineffective as practical guides to conduct, and always the compromises he achieved were dictated by his own profound and hardheaded knowledge of the nature of man. Thus, the author of the article in the *Encyclopaedia Britannica* to which I have referred recognizes that Johnson's position lies somewhere between the Hobbesian and Mandevillean conviction of total depravity and his own, that is, the author's, optimistic vision of human nature, which is obviously derived from Shaftesbury. Again, Johnson was moved by powerful humanitarian impulses, but he realized that the benevolism of his day lacked the sort of motive necessary to make it effective. The utilitarian thesis had a great appeal for him, but he knew that men are neither prudent nor foresighted enough to make it work on the basis of enlightened self-interest alone. Such examples could be multiplied indefinitely. This continual shoring up and reinforcing of the structure of his

---

[62] (Edinburgh), XII, 278.

moral notions to better fit them to the realities of human nature—his disregard of theoretical consistency—is largely responsible for that success which earned Johnson the title of "the first moralist of the age."

INDEX